THIS WAY TO CHANGE

POEMS · PROSE · PRACTICES

This Way to Change

a gentle guide to
personal transformation
and collective liberation

Jezz Chung

CHRONICLE PRISM

Library of Congress Cataloging-in-Publication Data
Names: Chung, Jezz, author.
Title: This way to change : a gentle guide to personal transformation and collective liberation / Jezz Chung.
Description: San Francisco, California : Chronicle Prism, [2023] | Includes bibliographical references.
Identifiers: LCCN 2023030507 (print) | LCCN 2023030508 (ebook) | ISBN 9781797226194 (hardcover) | ISBN 9781797226200 (ebook)
Subjects: LCSH: Change (Psychology) | Social change.
Classification: LCC BF637.C4 C48 2023 (print) | LCC BF637.C4 (ebook) | DDC 158.1--dc23/eng/20230707
LC record available at https://lccn.loc.gov/2023030507
LC ebook record available at https://lccn.loc.gov/2023030508

Manufactured in China.

Cover illustration by Jocelyn Tsaih.
Design by Pamela Geismar.
Typeset in Lust Display, Noah, and Minion Pro.

10 9 8 7 6 5 4 3 2 1

Chronicle books and gifts are available at special quantity discounts to corporations, professional associations, literacy programs, and other organizations. For details and discount information, please contact our premiums department at corporatesales@chroniclebooks.com or at 1-800-759-0190.

 CHRONICLE PRISM

Chronicle Prism is an imprint of
Chronicle Books LLC
680 Second Street
San Francisco, California 94107
www.chronicleprism.com

To the transformative, healing power of queer friendship

Transform yourself to transform the world.

— *Grace Lee Boggs*

[Boggs's quote] doesn't mean to get lost in the self, but rather to see our own lives and work and relationships as a front line, a first place we can practice justice, liberation, and alignment with each other and the planet.

— *adrienne maree brown*

A NOTE FROM THE AUTHOR

Change is a current. Like the weather, it's predictably unpredictable. It can strike suddenly like lightning or land slowly like flurries. Change hardens and softens us. It's something we endure and influence at the same time.

I began writing this book during a time of turbulence and transition in my life. In September 2020, less than a year into the global COVID-19 pandemic, I quit my job in advertising to prioritize my health and pursue my creative calling full time. After years of feeling burned out, excluded, and enraged in environments that weren't designed to support my success, I needed to reevaluate my life. Whose dreams was I helping to fulfill? What patterns of harm were I perpetuating? How much agency did I have in the life I was living—and was I even enjoying it day to day?

In many ways, these questions came out of a desire to heal. While studying race, gender, disability, power, and privilege, I was also studying trauma, astrology, psychology, neuroscience, lifestyle design, manifesting techniques, and metaphysics. I wanted to understand the roots of my pain and contribute to a world that makes us want to stay alive.

We are all used to shrinking ourselves and suppressing how we feel in one way or another. White-dominant heteronormativity and capitalist ableism hurt us all. The impact of oppression is a suppression of our imagination and a belief that a culture of inclusion, equity, access, and sustainability are impossible. Determining our values then becomes a compass to a different future.

As I oriented my life around my passions, interests, and curiosities, my world changed. I embraced more of my queerness and began identifying as nonbinary and genderfluid. I developed a different relationship with the idea of being Korean American. I began reframing my life through a neurodivergent lens and discovered that I'm autistic. I became a student of abolition and disability justice. And most profoundly, I learned how to love with fewer constraints and more freedom. Cultivating queer friendships in New York City during a time of crisis and fear taught me how to source care and safety among community and helped me generate hope during times of despair.

As you move through these poems, suggestions, and practices, let them guide you through the changes you're experiencing in your own life. Go through them alone or with friends. Note dates so you can reflect on your growth. Take breaks, pace your progress, and celebrate any shifts you feel along the way. Think of the words ahead as a map, each page a signpost guiding you toward the life you want to live, making a future of personal transformation and collective liberation more and more possible.

THIS DISTANCE

Throughout the pandemic, as COVID rates were spiking in New York City, I felt conflicted. Going outside meant putting myself and others at risk, while staying inside meant isolating until I became mad with loneliness. I felt hopeless and defeated trying to balance personal and collective safety. I wrote much of this section in a state of longing—what are the perspectives we're missing? What futures are available to me and the people I love? When you feel lost, turn to this section to know you're not moving through the distance alone.

HOW TO BUILD A WORLD

1. You begin by deciding
2. this is something I want to do
3. this one we're living in is too terrible
4. to continue with too much hierarchy
5. not enough ways to care
6. no regard for universal health.
7. You build a world by building relationships
8. with people who are also looking for
9. softness / somewhere to sit / some place to say
10. I'm struggling with this; I need help here.
11. You build a world by deciding this could be better
12. and by better, I mean safer and more secure and
13. more creative in the ways we survive.
14. You build a world by searching for
15. different ways to stay alive.

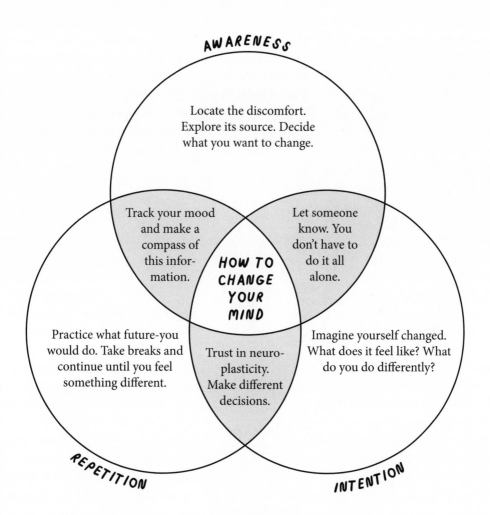

AWARENESS

Locate the discomfort. Explore its source. Decide what you want to change.

Track your mood and make a compass of this information.

Let someone know. You don't have to do it all alone.

HOW TO CHANGE YOUR MIND

Practice what future-you would do. Take breaks and continue until you feel something different.

Trust in neuroplasticity. Make different decisions.

Imagine yourself changed. What does it feel like? What do you do differently?

REPETITION

INTENTION

MY BEST MY VERY VERY BEST

the void
    doesn't call
        before it arrives

           each visit   a surprise
            "it's been a while!" it chimes
                  a while could mean days, weeks

        I wonder if I did something
      to prompt its arrival
    the mixed signals
I might have sent

        yes, I'm lonely   but not for you

        so   I move away to escape

    maybe this was its purpose
      a reason, a reminder

        my vocal coach says
            the opposite of tension is motion
           sway as you sing a hard note
             if it gets stuck
                spin your fingers
                  at your stomach
             imagine the air
           propelling your lungs
          let your voice follow

    I do this and
I pour smoother

ahhhhhhHHHHHH
 instead of
ahHhhHhhhhhh

        question—will it ever end?
    how long, this cycle?
        how thick, this time?

            I've been thinking in questions—

when does my desire for language
turn into an unhealthy obsession?
    am I catching up to words
        I haven't had access to?

            Asian American / Korean and American / first generation /
            neurodivergent / disabled / autistic / queer / nonbinary /
            genderfluid / pansexual / demisexual

or am I building cages
    to fly into from
        the one I'm in now

        I don't feel strong enough
    to roam in the open just yet

maybe this cage is a portal
    maybe this bird is already singing
        maybe this search is a melody

        this is my best
        this is my best

            my best is enough

            my best is always changing

this is my best
my best is enough

my best is always changing
if this is my best

will it ever feel like enough

LANGUAGE AS A LIMITATION, LANGUAGE AS A GENERATOR

In 1968, graduate students and life partners Yuji Ichioka and Emma Gee created the Asian American Political Alliance (AAPA) at the University of California, Berkeley, to bring together students of Chinese, Japanese, Filipinx, and other Asian diasporic descent.

This action for pan-Asian unity was inspired by the Black Power and anti-war movements organizing for political change. Cited by historians as the first organization to use the term "Asian American," the AAPA inspired the adoption of other acronyms used today, such as AAPI (Asian American and Pacific Islander) and AANHPI (Asian American and Native Hawaiian/Pacific Islander).

While naming ourselves is helpful for collective visibility, the acronyms don't convey the nuances of the people they aim to describe. How can a few letters carry the disparate cultural identities and roots of over fifty countries and hundreds of ethnic groups?

At the same time, organizing experiences into a shared racial identity and cultural label helps people find each other and unite under a similar vision to resist oppression, demand visibility, and determine a strategy for collective change. With ongoing anti-Asian violence and an urgency to voice issues that have long been ignored, we are at a critical time for evolving the idea of an "Asian American identity." Can such a thing even exist, or should we work to divest from the idea of singularity and focus more on creating solidarity among one another? Whose acceptance are we working to gain? I long for more expansive language to understand ourselves in relation to our history and in relation to one another. I wonder what could be made possible in this expansion.

WHERE ARE OUR ELDERS?

during the 1980s and 90s
people in positions
of political power
let thousands of people die
because they were afraid of
the growing visibility
of queerness, of
a pleasure revolution

I learn about this from
watching shows
reading books
searching phrases
collecting language
I learn about this
because there are
no queer elders
around me
who teach me
what it means to live
as part of a legacy

they severed a connection
to people who could have
taught us about ourselves

a whole generation
of ancestors missing

an entire era of elders
framed like suicide

they called it a health epidemic
called it an act of nature

call it a god complex
call it what it is

call it—negligence
call it—murder
call it—the government
killing our ancestors

MAKING HISTORY

History isn't something outside us. It's something we build every day through what we believe and what we do. This is easy to forget, so we often place the responsibility of history-making on someone else. Growing up in a conservative, Christian, Korean immigrant home, I wasn't taught how to think critically. I was taught to accept authority without protest. I was shut down when I asked questions and was told to be quiet when I got excited. There were no introductions to queer history in my public school curriculums in Atlanta and Houston, and there were no culturally and politically engaged elders in my family who I could learn from.

So I taught myself. I read about the work of New York City's LGBTQIA+ champions, like Marsha P. Johnson and Sylvia Rivera, who resisted the NYPD's now-illegal policing of queer community spaces. I sought out more queer stories in film, television, art, and literature, and I learned about the legacy of state-sponsored violence, neglect, and erasure of our communities. I saw the impact of our government's lack of care for disabled and immuno-compromised people during the COVID-19 pandemic and the ways it mirrored the Reagan administration's hostile neglect of queer people during the AIDS epidemic.

The pattern has been clear: During a health crisis, the people who suffer most are the people who have been deemed the least worthy of protection. People who are poor, working class, of color, disabled, and queer are caught in a systemic cycle of harm.

We often blame individuals for their circumstances. Why don't you work harder? Why aren't you healthier? Why do you need so much help? Why are you so angry? This is the conditioning of ableism and racism.

What if we looked deeper and asked different questions? Why don't people have access to the healthcare and support they need? Why are certain communities targeted, blamed, and excluded while others accumulate privilege?

The pandemic has illuminated our underlying beliefs about what kind of people are considered disposable. As infuriating as these revelations are, they also present an opportunity to change our collective patterns.

History is a part of us. It's not static, but living, something we shape every day. Learning about our lineage helps us understand how we got to where we are now and gives us the knowledge and vocabulary to write a better future.

●●

YOUR PERSONAL HISTORY

Think about the legacy of your life so far. Think about the people who have impacted you and the people you have impacted. Think about the milestones you're proud of reaching. Then, think about these moments through the lens of community, care, and liberation. For example, maybe you're proud of building a support system of chosen family. Maybe you feel accomplished from learning about the history of your cultural identity. Perhaps you come from a family history of abuse and you're breaking cycles by healing the way you sustain relationships.

Think about your lineage. Not just the lineage of your given family, but the lineage of your values and the rituals of your chosen community. What people—whether those you know or those you admire from afar—have influenced you? What cultural moments have shaped your life? What experiences have helped you grow?

Make a timeline or a tree with some of these key figures and events. Remind yourself that your life exists within a world bigger than yours, but that you, too, influence the world around you. Let this connection between the personal and the collective be a framework that shapes the way you think about your legacy.

●●

FUTURE PARABLE

the pandemic begins and
Parable of the Sower becomes
a popular escape, much like
Animal Crossing becomes
an obsession, maybe
some of the hiding
is in the immersing

Octavia's world
a premonition of ours
or ours a premonition of hers
she warns us in her stories
of a time when survival
turns us against each other

what is a warning when
you're receiving it too late?

                                      a testimony

as I was reading
I became Lauren
I dreamed as Lauren
I moved as Lauren
my pain became hers
I mean her pain
became mine

hyperempathy activated
full-body sensations
is it safe to have
this much imagination?

what is the diagnosis
for when care consumes logic

when overextending is genetic
baked into bone behavior
when you see everyone
as someone who needs saving
when you make it a mission
to solve other people's stories
when you're frozen with
someone else's fear

an elder in Chinatown carrying
gallons of plastic bottles
a cyclist pedaling through
wind and snow
videos of people
hanging on to planes
shoved off departing trains

people who
didn't have the
choice to escape

people who
didn't have a
choice but to escape

the future is calling for our help
and most of us are too afraid to listen

ANXIETY AS AN ACTIVE USE OF IMAGINATION

Since early childhood, I've experienced panic attacks. On planes, at malls, in bathrooms. At work, at parties, day and night. With strangers, with friends, and by myself—which is when they feel the scariest.

It's disorienting. I forget how to breathe, and I feel like I'm about to die for no apparent reason. Logic does little to calm my worries, and I suddenly become a screenwriter for a horror movie starring me—thrashing within a series of worst-case scenarios.

Anxiety often stems from our traumas. We experience life as an accumulation of information, and sometimes this information sits inside us as unprocessed pain. This gnaws at our sense of safety and tells us we should always be on the lookout for danger. It's a survival mechanism gone into overdrive.

But anxiety is also an expression of our imagination, a reminder that we have the ability to dream up different realities. Anxiety is also a reminder that we care—about this conversation coming up, about showing up for someone or something we love, about the future of this place we inhabit. How clever and caring it is to be anxious.

Maybe there's a way to reroute this creativity. Maybe there's a way to notice when anxiety is talking—through diabolic, catastrophic scenarios—and redirect this act of imagination to scenarios that involve us doing well, being supported, and feeling good.

ALL THE TIMES I'VE WANTED TO

age 7, panic on a plane
lungs stopped
or so I thought
my body becomes
a spectacle, I learn
my fear is a source
of embarrassment

age 9, watching my
parents fly apart
not knowing who
to believe

age 11, I dig streams into skin
the only blood I've never
been afraid of is my own

age 13, Alex ends his life
and I want to join him
thinking, leaving must be
easier than enduring
I learn, 엄마 doesn't know
how to hold me when I cry

age 14, my best friend ghosts me
on the school steps with no ride home
I learn, people are very skilled at lying
and I am very skilled at believing

ages 18 to 22, I try sex like the others do
I learn, no one is falling as fast as I am

I learn, I'm a deep sea diver
looking for love in shallow waters

age 24, I think I want to be
an advertising executive
I learn the payment of pretending
pulls me into deeper debt

age 27, crying at the grocery store
a sign I need to go far away, again

29, I'm timed like wine
this loneliness has
a diagnosis, a direction
I'm autistic, I'm an artist
storytelling is a calling

age 30, I'm sculpting
doorways inside this darkness
this digging, this depth
was always a way
to come back home

METHOD TO MAP THE FUTURE

1. Tune into your body.
2. Search for signals.
3. Reflect. What patterns? What drivers?
4. Study the current conditions.
5. Look for evidence supporting the world you want to see.
6. Find a way to contribute to movements for change.
7. Adapt and evolve your idea of what makes a movement.
8. Treat it like an iterative creative process.
9. Do what you can, when you can, how you can.
10. Repeat.

IF SADNESS IS A SEASON

then this loneliness   a priming, a pruning
    a coming and going   a practice in longing
        a continuing, dying   reinventing, a life with
            more living than this   there must be more
                than this season   than this grieving

                the version of me who had no entry into community
        still lives within me   fights to stay, to linger

      I sometimes get stuck in the giving   of goodbye

I want to nurture this Jezz too   *thank them for surviving*

the Jezz who didn't see a future   the Jezz who wanted to
      empty onto   train tracks

           calculating

        how much would it hurt

      how long would it take

but never actually   going through

because there are too many people to love
too many I've yet to meet   too many stories to tell

        I want to comfort this Jezz too

this, a history lesson
meaning, my body
           still pulses with memories
                in isolation
            in irritation
          thinking
        everyone

        has somebody to hold
        everyone falls asleep with
        the satisfaction of being held
                 everyone
                 except me

but wait!
this is no longer my reality
    my reality is now
        many hands to hold
        many people to call
        many invitations to get and give
        many arms to pinch*
           my reality is now
                cuddle puddles with friends
                dinner dates many times a week
                conversation for hours
                supporting each other's projects
                listening to each other's frustrations
                showing up over and over again
                freedom dreaming**
                together

this is now my reality

what do you do when you turn your dreams into a destination
when the fear of not having is no longer driving you
when you become a different story

when this season passes, as all seasons do
look back
                    and learn to love this Jezz too

* Pinching arms is one of my favorite stims. Stimming is a self-soothing technique that many neurodivergent people do.

** Coined by historian, scholar, and professor Robin D. G. Kelley, author of *Freedom Dreams: The Black Radical Imagination.*

YOUR BODY IS A PLACE

Think of your body as a map. Every location, conversation, feeling, person, and experience is a site marked throughout sections of your skin—some marks are shallow, some are deep, some are pleasant, and some are excruciating to revisit. Healing from trauma requires a slow, patient reckoning of all the places you've been and a declaration of where you want to go.

This is terrifying work! To connect the dots of our fears and decide we want something different from what we know is like going off-road into an abyss. Hypervigilance says, "There are so many things that can go wrong! What if we get hurt? What if dreaming big only leads to big disappointment? What if we end up somewhere worse than where we began?"

Life is too much to navigate alone. Through our relationships, we give each other rides to new destinations and expand our view of what's possible. We help each other recover when we break down on the side of the road, and we remind each other of the progress we've made.

Next time you feel activated or shut down after visiting a site of trauma, try a somatic exercise to tune into your body and care for this inner landscape you inhabit. The next page has a guided exercise to help you drive gently on this journey. Imagine planting some gardens along your route, complete with hammocks and cozy cushions—safe places to rest while you take in the view.

VISUALIZING SAFETY

Therapy—in its various forms—helps me practice feeling safer and freer in my body. This exercise is adapted from something I learned in talk therapy to address anxiety. Somatically, anxiety shows up for me as a racing heartbeat, tight shoulders, weight under my brows, and difficulty breathing. This practice can help you recalibrate your body and ease your mind through the power of visualization.

Picture a place of safety—somewhere comfortable, somewhere you feel at ease. It can be somewhere you've been before or somewhere imaginary. What do you see? What do you smell? What do you hear? What do you feel? What textures are around you, what colors, what temperature?

Breathe into this visual slowly and deeply.

Think of a single word to describe this place. I often come back to the word "secure."

Repeat the word as you record this feeling in your body. Know that every time you recall this sensation, you strengthen your ability to access it. This place is always within you to come back to when you need it.

DREAMING OF BILLIE

I dreamt of Billie Eilish last night
Billie and me, on a bed

harmonizing in pajamas
streaming live! on the internet

in this dream, I'm bracing
myself for what Billie is thinking

am I saying the right things
being the right friend

I fear I'll lose my right to be here
I fear I'll bore her, I fear I'll offend

and I hate that I dreamt this
because I could have dreamt of

anything, anyone else
and my dreams landed on her

which means as much as I
demand myself to decolonize

my subconscious has
different literacy
white supremacy so
potent I can hardly taste it

subconscious still influenced
by the social currency

of someone like Billie whose
mom taught her how to write songs

whose dad taught her how to play instruments
whose brother is a built-in collaborator

who had the tools the space
the support the resources

the circumstances to become
the star Billie is to practice the genius

Billie has because I believe everyone
has genius inside of them it's mostly

a matter of how much access you have
to practice it, to perform it, to get to know it

my subconscious knows this currency matters
so as much as I try to opt out of payments

as much as I liberate my mind
decolonize my body*

I know access to my dreams
depends on this proximity

this isn't a dream about Billie
it's about the gravity of whiteness

the way it cycles and recycles
the way it grants and gatekeeps

the way it distorts access, talent, success
and how even someone like Billie

who opts out of her own payments
wears gender expansive clothing

turns experimental bedroom songs
into radio hits, even someone like her

represents the borders of
dreams I may never meet

* "Decolonizing the Body" is a six-week course created and facilitated by somatic practitioner Kelsey Blackwell. Participating in this communal learning helped me further embody the practice of decolonizing—divesting from the systemic beliefs and behaviors of Eurocentric white supremacy, heteropatriarchy, ableism, and capitalism, while investing in a practice of sourcing power from within the wisdom of my lineage and nature, and from my own experiences.

DECONSTRUCT WITHOUT DESTROYING YOURSELF

Resisting white supremacy is exhausting. No matter how many books you read, infographics you save, and conversations you have, the mechanisms of white supremacy are designed to repeat themselves in ways beyond individual influence. We are intricately interconnected, yes. We have a responsibility to actively unlearn racism, yes. But it is impossible to personally take on the mission of undoing the damages of a persistently fueled and thoroughly funded system.

As poet Scott Woods put it in a 2014 essay, "It's like being born into air; you take it in as soon as you breathe. . . . It is a thing you have to keep scooping out of the boat of your life to keep from drowning in it."

Racism is tangled into everything we experience. We inhale the language, the imagery, the jokes and subtext, and we perpetuate them with our every exhalation. Accepting this is part of the challenge of change. Without acknowledging this reality, we can drive ourselves mad wondering why "the work" isn't working for us. White supremacy is woven into the fabric of our collective consciousness, and as people committed to change, we sometimes turn this fabric into a cape. We believe that we must become martyrs for justice, present ourselves as perfect practitioners of fairness and equity. This is too much pressure for anyone to bear.

Unraveling the thread of this fabric involves intention and iteration. History and memory are both personal and collective. As you collect resources and techniques to practice the work of decolonizing, understand that it is not your responsibility to uphold the most morally sound, anti-oppressive perspective of all time, at all times.

Fault and fumble. Learn from the mess-ups. Transformative justice teaches us to move away from a culture of punishment and into a culture of compassion and care—something we can practice within ourselves.

Turn decolonization into an ongoing series of destinations and navigate patiently, at a pace that works for you. Maintain the vision of the world you want without punishing yourself for not living up to it all the time. Transformation is a process, not an end point.

● ●

WHERE DO YOU SOURCE YOUR POWER?

Voice-note, write, type, or doodle your responses to these prompts. Email them to yourself or print them out and keep them in an envelope with today's date written on the front. Set a reminder in your calendar to revisit your notes six months from now and explore what has shifted and changed.

In what ways do you notice yourself enacting a sense of dominance or hierarchy over people in your life?

Go to whitesupremacyculture.info and read the piece "White Supremacy Culture" by Tema Okun. What characteristics of white supremacy culture do you notice within yourself and the professional and personal spaces you inhabit? Note specific examples. Choose one or two of these traits to work on shifting, pacing yourself with patience.

What does power mean to you?

Where do you think your power comes from?

How do you respond when other people make mistakes?

When was the last time you punished yourself for being imperfect?

● ●

CONFESSIONS

I am clumsy with conversation.
I am either silent or spilling.
I think I'm so damaged that I'm dangerous
to everyone around me. My body thinks
danger exists everywhere I go. I'm tired
of being exhausted and what if it's
because I'm from the future.* I've been
in a relationship with a married man.
He was poly. His wife was not (aware).
I left when I stopped wanting to be a secret.
I've wanted married women to kiss me.
Fuck the institution of marriage but I still
dream of it. I dream of being wanted so
madly that someone wants to try forever
with me. I am shy when I am in wanting.
I am shy because I am afraid.
I am afraid because I am used to
wanting and not being wanted back.
Every day I wake up it's a magic trick.
I am driven by the fears of my
mother's mother's mother and so on.
I can't sleep when I'm hungry.
I am always hungry, I am never
hungry. I dream of being someone's
hunger. Did I mention, I dream so often
I lose track of reality. I have a pattern of
sharing too much, too quickly. My therapist
says I treat friendship like a crash course.
Take notes. Study. Test. Pass/Fail.

My impatience to learn people gets
in the way of my pleasure of knowing people.
I am enamored by my friends until they
become annoying. I fear every friendship has
an expiration date. I don't believe in
miracles but I believe in myself.
I believe in miracles but I don't
believe in myself.

I forget feelings very easily.
I am terrified that one day, all
my lovers will decide I'm too
autistic—I mean needy—to
love. I wonder if I am only
lovable from a distance.
I wonder if I only know
how to love from a distance.

It's hard for me to weather people.
I resent how much I have to practice
forgiveness, probably a disability trauma.
Probably because, like I said, I'm from the
future where ableism has been abolished.
I never waste money on books
which is why I buy so many.
Pages are easier to turn to than people.
I am a layered cake of compassion and cruelty.

I fear I will never find family
(lasting kinship) because I lose
myself in intimacy, because what if my
brain cannot handle the amount of
closeness required to become family.

I am angry at my extroverted and
neuronormative** friends. I wonder if
they are getting more out of life than me.
Which is to say, I wonder if they find it
easier to   access joy.

If community is sustained through consistency,
what if I can't show up next time. I fear
I'll never catch up to all the drinking, the
all-night dancing, all the things my body can't do.

I fear my experiences are not grand enough
to be written, to be read, to exist as an archive.
Which is to say, I'm not grand enough to exist
in this time. I fear I'll give up on being alive.

I fear I'm being left behind.

Am I the only one who wants to leave?

Why am I the only one
thinking out loud
here, right now.

* This idea stems from the theory that disabled people are from the future. See societyofdisabledoracles.com and Leah Lakshmi Piepzna-Samarasinha's book *The Future Is Disabled*.

** "Neuronormative" refers to someone with a brain that doesn't differ from a dominant and acceptable way of functioning that upholds hyperproductivity and respectability. In contrast, people who are autistic or live with ADHD, dyslexia, and/or other disabilities are considered neurodivergent.

REVERSE THIS SPELL

SURPRISE!

a crying spell
a waterworks attack
SURPRISE!
sinking, again
SURPRISE!
suddenly numb with
everything you hate
about your life

Ren Hang
stationed friends
on roofs
in bedrooms
with snakes
and phone chords

stacked bodies
like butterflies
lips parted
red like censor
red like country
the art is in
the performance

the invention
is in the way you
remain alive

Ren Hang, 2017, age 30
decided to end his life

two years before he left
he wrote: "Every morning
I wake up wondering
why I am still alive."

each time I read
about someone
who ends their life
I promise myself
I will not end my
life as a surprise
I will devote myself
to the conditions
that keep us alive

FEELINGS AS SEASONS

Buddhist teachings encourage us to think of feelings like clouds passing by in the sky. Separating our sense of self from the ebb and flow of emotional turbulence helps us see emotions as temporary sensations so we don't become too attached to a single state of mind.

This kind of emotional regulation is an embodied practice, meaning it takes time for the body to learn what the mind might grasp more quickly. Feelings are loud. They consume attention. They spill over onto the people around us. What if we imagined depression and anxiety like they were weather patterns to adapt to? What if it's normal for the body to slow down and need an umbrella, extra warmth, more fresh air, or hibernation to adapt to the conditions of our changing inner world? Instead of blaming ourselves, what if we adjusted our care?

Loneliness, sadness, anger—think of them as temperatures. Feel without adding value judgments of good or bad, right or wrong. Even when it doesn't feel like it, we're growing from the information our emotions provide. Let your learnings influence the next season of you.

GIVE ME STRENGTH TO SURF THE LENGTH OF THIS LIGHT

this sadness could swallow me
this sadness could martyr me
a pair of tinted glasses
a mighty slob
a slow siren
a maple muzzle

this sadness, a state of being
a country enforcing borders
rejecting all visitors

this sadness, a temperature
with boiling point
always changing

this sadness, a fickle duet
bagpipes with no harmony
a debt always asking to be
collected like here, take this
memory and twist it until
it only exists as pity

this sadness has no point
only sharp corners
this sadness keeps me in
won't let me out

      this sadness, a slow chewing

         this sadness is to be washed out of hair
        to be stuffed into pillows
          to be watered and weeded

this sadness, a stagnant growing
this slowness, a steady moving

this sadness
a hallowed type of surfing

this sadness
a pulsing type of pleasure
if you let it keep breathing

DISABILITY, DIAGNOSIS, AND CHOICE

Disability, as a collective definition, is difficult to unpack. I used to be afraid of this word. I thought "disabled" was a slur, something I wasn't allowed to say, much less claim for myself. When I began making disabled friends and engaging in dialogue about the disability justice movement, I doubted my instincts. Am I allowed to be a part of this movement? How would my world change with these frameworks? I started identifying as disabled in private, reading perspectives from disabled people and journaling about our similarities. I began going to events run by disabled artists and organizers. The more safety I felt within these community spaces, the more comfortable I became openly discussing my disabled experiences.

Among disability advocates, there's an ongoing discussion about the medical model of disability and the social model of disability. The medical model of disability is our current status quo—medical conditions explain a person's physical and intellectual differences, and we provide support through medicine and policy. The social model of disability, coined by disabled academic Mike Oliver, offers an alternative perspective where we place the disability not on the individual, but on the larger social structures we live within. Under the social model, it isn't someone's differences that make them disabled, but the social and cultural impairments and lack of accommodations that result in disabled experiences.

In my personal journey, I've found myself bouncing between and among both models. Working a corporate job in my twenties gave me access to healthcare benefits and allowed me to secure a diagnosis from a clinical psychiatrist. But as much as I thought this language of diagnosis would free me, it tempted me to define my life by my disabilities. Much of Western medicine is rooted in white supremacy, patriarchy, and capitalism. Even the medical term "mental illness" is an extension of oppressive language. I'm frustrated that I need to speak this language to get the care I need. Discovering the social model of disability helped me develop a sense of autonomy and reimagine care through a liberated, anti-oppressive framework. This helps me think beyond the choices offered by the dominant culture (psychiatrist, diagnosis, pharmaceutical intervention) and advocate for awareness and access to more choices (holistic approaches, herbalism and plants, traditional Chinese medicine, psychedelic therapy, energetic healing, community-based crisis intervention). Studying the neurodiversity movement and the autistic self-advocacy movement taught me alternatives to a pathology-based approach and offered more compassionate perspectives. What if mental illnesses are actually just mental differences? What if we treat these differences as something to understand and adjust to instead of shame and punish? What if we saw symptoms of individual mental illness as effects of collective trauma? What if we don't even need the language of disability someday because our world is designed in a way that considers physical and intellectual diversity?

We have the power to design a future where everyone gets the care they need. In this future, we all have access to the medicine we deserve, without having to fight for it. While we continue to push for structural change, including universal healthcare, I wish for more of us to expand our understanding of disability to free ourselves from the idea that diagnosis is the only choice.

I NEED A DIFFERENT DOCTOR

Mom, I have ADHD.
Mom, I heard it in school.
Mom, we need to go see a doctor.
No, a real doctor. Not the pastor, not the
church friend, not this knockoff Kumon tutor.
Mom, I don't know what insurance is because
Mom, you never explain things to me and

Mom, I know you can barely understand yourself
and you don't know how to say Suji-ya, I'm doing
the best I can and I don't know about the medical
industrial complex and its agenda to make people
dependent on pills instead of changing the
conditions that make us need them and

Mom, it's getting harder for me and
I know school is supposed to be hard
but is it supposed to be THIS hard.
Mom, I keep reading the same thing
over and over again and it doesn't make sense
and I know I'm in the "gifted class" but
why am I always the last to turn my test in.

Mom, I appreciate you turning everything into art
like the time I fell asleep and you stayed up till 4
staining and burning the edges of my project
so it looked like the real constitution and

Mom, I know we're trying to find ourselves in this history and
Mom, I know you try to teach me about Korea and how

North became North and South became South and why
everyone looks slightly Japanese in our family and

Mom, I don't understand debt so I don't understand
why we're moving all the time. Mom, I'm depressed and
no I'm not being dramatic when I say I have trouble breathing.
Mom, I don't understand why I can't keep any friends.
Mom, none of this church is helping.
Mom, I've already tried talking to god
but I think I need medicine beyond prayer.
I think I need to get far away from here.
Somewhere people believe me when I say
I like boys and girls and both and neither.
Somewhere people believe me when I say
I want to do it all and do it in ways it hasn't been
done before. Somewhere I can make something
living and breathing from all this dying.
Mom, I feel like I'm always dying.

Mom, I'm autistic and I'm pretty sure it runs in the family.
Mom, how have we survived so far without this language.
Mom, this is why every time I dig myself into another world
I'm amazed at all the times I decided to keep myself alive.

AN ODE TO BEING NEEDY

Being disabled in an ableist society requires an exhausting and sometimes dehumanizing level of disclosure. We are taught that asking for anything other than the default is too much hassle, so we're often placed in situations where we have to educate someone about our experiences in order to get our needs met. At the same time, advocating for accommodations is a practice of reclaiming agency, especially for those of us who have been historically disempowered. Every time we ask for something we need, we are improving our collective quality of life. We've been taught to expect and be satisfied with the bare minimum—but we need and deserve more than that.

A body is not something to be fixed; it is something to be tended to, supported, and collaborated with. Understanding this makes way for a more compassionate relationship with the accommodations we need.

Whether you identify as disabled or not, make a list of your access needs— the things that reduce stress and create comfort for you, the things that help you show up with more ease.

HOW TO IDENTIFY THE ACCESS YOU NEED

Think of access as the conditions that support your capacity to participate with both physical and psychological safety. Access is a form of inclusion. While we think of access as something that is exclusively for disabled people, access is something everyone needs. Advocating for access and promoting its presence elevates the experience for everybody. Ask yourself: *Can I safely and comfortably enter, move through, and communicate within this space?*

Consent

Am I actively agreeing to what is happening in this experience? Is there a part of this I'm being pressured into? Do I understand the general expectations?

Agency

Am I being seen, heard, and valued for my presence? Do I feel comfortable contributing my perspective?

Choice

Beyond what works for most people, are there other options that work for me? Are there points of check-in where I can express what I need?

● ●

DREAM UP SOMETHING DIFFERENT

Many social gatherings can feel unwelcoming for disabled and neuro-divergent people. Loud music, multiple conversations at once, or a lack of food options can cause people to feel excluded and overstimulated. The more I learned about my neurodivergence, the more difficult it became for me to endure the discomfort of trying to fit myself into normative spaces. Have you felt left out or out of place recently? What would have helped you feel more comfortable? If you were organizing the gathering, what would you do differently?

Design your ideal gathering in as much sensory detail as you can think of. What does it feel like when you get there? What sounds or vibrations are there—or is it silent? Who is there? What are you wearing, what are you doing? Are you sitting, dancing, lying down? What kind of conversations are you having? What are you eating or drinking?

The next time you're in a space that isn't designed with your needs or comfort in mind, conjure the experience of this ideal gathering. Write out scripts to reference the next time you're asking for something different than what's being offered. *Example: I want to be at the dinner party, but I'm not feeling very social lately. Do you have a quiet place where I can take some breaks throughout the evening?*

● ●

OKAY, I'M NOT OKAY

every day
I wake up not okay
everything from then
becomes a game
of feeling a little less not okay

okay, maybe I can meditate
okay, maybe I can drink tea
okay, maybe I can eat something

this game of
okay/not okay
exhausts me

as I write, edit, email
negotiate, advocate, ruminate
read, journal, spill, save
rest, forget, remember

repeat repeat repeat

as I fight for approval from
younger versions of myself
who had less access
to who they were

I'm shouting back
we're better now!
we're not where we were
and this is enough to celebrate

I'm growing and itching in this shape

the future feels too heavy to happen
so I set it down and travel into the past

every night
when the sun goes down
my body holds a funeral
I ache like I've given birth to a day

so I am learning to let the okay die
release it into the night
let the moon turn me over

okay, again

LONELINESS IS A REMINDER OF HOW UNIQUE YOU ARE

You will experience grief, rage, sorrow, doubt, and confusion throughout your lifetime. And in a way, you'll go through these feelings alone. Loneliness is a reminder of how uniquely alive you are. At the same time, there are people willing to experience grief, rage, sorrow, doubt, and confusion alongside you. There are people ready to be lonely with you.

One of the most damaging aspects of trauma and oppression is how they isolate us. Racism, sexism, and ableism have compounding effects on our psyche—they tell us it's not okay to be vulnerable and honest about where we are and what we're experiencing. But we don't need to reach a certain level of healing or success to be lovable. Part of the practice of decolonization is loving ourselves as we are and seeing our bodies as changing ecosystems instead of fixed machines.

If you are longing for a life of connection and community, but loneliness is your current reality, consider this: What if loneliness is part of your journey? What if this feeling is shaping your life's direction? Believe that there are communities (plural!) of friends, lovers, neighbors, and collaborators who are also journeying out of their isolation and ready to meet you where you are. As you learn to love and accept the parts of yourself that feel too scary, too ugly to be shared, these parts become portals to deeper connections.

Some parts of the healing process are done alone, but so much of healing is done within the practice of relating to one another. Developing compassion for ourselves in our states of loneliness is a profound way of accepting the unique, complex, and universal feelings of what it means to be fully human. And this compassion helps us meet ourselves and others with less judgment and more understanding.

MOTHER-DAUGHTER

how do you know when you're about to cry?
- like a boiling in the chest
- like a pinching in the face
- like a sweltering in the skin underneath

엄마 said
I'm sorry I could not love you better

I feel like a terrible daughter
for not knowing how to accept
her apology so I say sorry back
I'm sorry we are so far apart
I'm sorry I enjoy this distance
I'm sorry I may never understand
I'm sorry our love has always
been lost in translation
too distorted within
generational, cultural,
religious differences

I'm sorry that I wonder
if I am chronically lonely
because I've never been
known by the people
who have known me
the longest

I'm sorry
I don't know
how to let myself
be known by you

to feel alone is
to feel unknown

to feel alone is
to feel unknown

to feel alone is
to feel unknown

INTRODUCTION TO ABOLITION

During the summer of 2020, millions of Americans organized to protest ongoing patterns of state violence. Largely catalyzed by the murder of George Floyd by a Minneapolis police officer, resonators of the Black Lives Matter movement called for a divestment of funds from traditional police forces—and an investment in community care resources. Rage against the government took physical shape in the form of large-scale, widespread demonstrations. The message was clear: We must dismantle the structures that hurt us. The growing movement for prison and police abolition urges us to consider: If we burn it all down, what will we build in its place?

Studying abolition and transformative justice has taught me to question violence from a systemic and cultural angle. Prisons and police were created within a white supremacist power structure to maintain racial hierarchy. Our systems punish people for circumstances those same systems force them into. This mindset of policing and punishment trickles down into how we treat one another. So how do we stop this cycle? How do we learn to abolish the cop in our head?*

A step: Forgive ourselves for our learned carceral (punitive, punishing) thinking.

Another step: Consider a different approach, one that enacts less control over what people do and brings more curiosity about why they're doing it.

Another step: Understand that there is no stopping—the trying becomes the failing becomes the doing. Remember, perfectionism is a symptom of white supremacy culture. No one has to be perfect to be worthy of care.

* A tweet by artist, author, and filmmaker Tourmaline on June 7, 2020, reads: "When we say abolish police. We also mean the cop in your head and in your heart."

TRANSFORMING A CYCLE OF HARM INTO A CYCLE OF CARE

culture designed to uplift and protect a select few while leaving many without their basic needs met

a person stuck in this cycle experiences systemic harm over time

a harmed (abused, neglected, traumatized) person with unmet needs causes another person harm through violence/ abuse

INTERRUPTING THE CYCLE

address the conditions that create violence, inequity, inaccessibility, and exclusion

look to nature for examples of abundance and interdependence

develop a more generative relationship to the land we live on and organize a sustainable flow of resources among one another

develop a more generative relationship to one another and there is no longer a need to cause excessive harm to get our needs met

WHAT MADE THE VILLAIN?

what conditions make a villain?
how many unanswered
howls for help until
a villain believes: control
is the only way to achieve

how much can someone
endure before suffering
becomes default

we have more ways of harming
than we do of healing
(why / do we believe this?)

Toni Cade Bambara:
. . . as a cultural worker who
belongs to an oppressed people
my job is to make revolution irresistible. . . .

what if pain is more profitable
and what if profit is too high
a currency to resist

please! we need softer ways to resist
please! we must make a sensation of care
the way violence is a tempting spectacle

Inspired by an excerpt from the 1970 documentary *Meeting the Man: James Baldwin in Paris*, in which Baldwin speaks of love as a movement that holds the world together. Rather than falling into despair, he urges us to remember, "Everyone you're looking at is also you. . . .You could be that monster, you could be that cop. And you have to decide, in yourself, not to be."

TOUGH TRUTHS

1. You can't control people into loving you.
2. Control is a power-hungry illusion.
3. You can't be friends with everyone you meet.
   Meaning you cannot be liked (or loved, for that matter)
   by everyone who meets you.
   Meaning there are many different places to meet.
4. Too much sweetness can cause love to sour
   (you can overdose on hope).
5. It feels unbearable right before a breakthrough.

THIS IS A WAR YOU CAN WIN

when the loud is quiet
when the quiet is loud
when conversations are a chore
when the thing takes over
when you're drowning in the day
when breathing becomes
a battle no one can see

turn silence into a song
conversations into celebrations
take the thing and flip it over
kick paddle stroke
swim swim don't stop just swim
this is a war you can win

IF I WERE TO DESCRIBE MY DEPRESSION TO YOU

it feels like a pit
the inside of something chewy
searching for softness
but the more you bite
the deeper you get
under skin you remember
you need more to survive
so you keep biting
and softness hardens
and the fruit becomes
a thirst for something different
something better something more
so you keep drinking
and drinking and drinking
and the thirst never goes away
it hides and returns at random

I've been thinking
about this book a lot
Lost Connections:
Why You're Depressed
and How to Find Hope
by Johann Hari
a book I read in a desperate attempt
to end my life-ending thoughts
I wanted a reason to stay alive
and this pitting
this experience that
medical practitioners call

major depression
this parasite that
WebMD describes as
hopeless thinking, fatigue,
changes in appetite
this thing that impacts
millions of us, apparently
depression can be peeled
down to one core cause:
<u>disconnection</u>
from nature
from purpose
from values
from community
from knowing ourselves

the summer of 2020
a clear message emerged:
in order to survive
as a collective body
<u>we must divest from harm</u>
<u>and invest in care</u>
we must disconnect from harm
we must connect to care
practice our potential
to live beyond ourselves

so yes, I'll chew on this core
held in place by
a body of memories
within these routes underground

this mycelium network*
of information shared across miles
mountains rivers and oceans

we are tendrils, thoughts
connected to each other
one affects the quality
of another's life
acts of love come from
behaviors come from beliefs of love
remember, we can
choose love again and again
remember, it's never too late
for another choice
kindness a cure
community an antidote

and this is how you turn a fruit into a tree
this is how you turn a pit into a well

pour from this source to remember why you are alive

* The documentary *Fantastic Fungi* explains how mycelium, or mushrooms, are some of
the original sources of intelligence in our living ecosystem. They survive through an under-
ground network of complex roots that share information about what and how much is safe
to consume. This is how trees depend on one another for survival.

THROUGH THE VOID

I've started to think of my depressive episodes as "the void." When the void takes over, a sense of emptiness and doom consumes me. In this haze, life lacks meaning and hope disappears from view. Seemingly simple tasks like brushing my teeth, eating a meal, or taking a shower feel daunting and drain me of the little energy I have.

As much as I try to fight it or reach for a way out, sometimes I just have to swim in it. My sadness becomes a river to float through, instead of a problem to fix.

There's a delicate balance between indulgence and acceptance. I give myself permission to feel bad without letting this state of mind define the trajectory of my life. I dream of the day the trips into the void become lighter in weight and shorter in length. To get there, I'm learning to give myself over to the pain, knowing that I've already survived the void for decades.

When things feel too grim to bear and I buckle under the weight of the day, I sometimes turn to a technique I learned in a breathwork class: 1. A sharp inhale through the mouth, expanding the belly. 2. Another sharp inhale through the mouth, now expanding the chest. 3. A long exhale out of the mouth. Combining this with a mantra, like "This is temporary," helps me separate myself from what I'm feeling.

WHY WE'RE AFRAID OF OURSELVES

COLONIALISM
SLAVERY
POLICE & PRISONS
CULTURE OF
PUNISHMENT
SELF-PERCEPTION

A fear of rejection (abandonment,
betrayal, shamed for being "different")
causes us to suppress our emotions
and our need to connect.

CULTURE OF
HYPER-
INDEPENDENCE
AND
PERFECTIONISM

*Then, what if we were all a little more honest about
our fears, wants, and needs, accepting where we are
without judgment (good/bad, right/wrong)?
What would this undo within us?
What would this do for our collective sense of safety?*

● ●

GIVING DIRECTION TO DEPRESSION

How would you describe your depression?

Are there any cultural or systemic influences to your sadness?

What do you think this sadness is trying to tell you?

If you could change the conditions of your life right now,
what would you change?

Is there a way to advocate for a degree of this change
in the spaces you're in?

What do you want to stop carrying alone?

● ●

FEELINGS AS NAVIGATION

Feelings are vital sources of information that guide our decision-making processes. When we're disassociated, we don't know how to tune into these signals. Trauma takes us out of our bodies as a protective mechanism. If our consent has been violated in the past or we weren't allowed to practice agency growing up, we may not feel safe listening to our body's subtle cues. Reconnecting with our body's languages connects us to our intuition, our internal compass. Should I move forward? Should I step back? Will this support me? Is this someone I want to be in relationship with?

My body sends me clear signals when I don't want to be in conversation with someone. I've learned not to place the blame on the person. Sometimes, I'm tired and don't have enough left in my social battery to engage. Sometimes, I don't feel safe because of the language they use and the undertones of racism, sexism, or ableism in what they're saying. Other times, I simply don't want to make the effort to connect.

Once, a friend asked me how to decode someone's intentions. How to know when to continue engaging and when to set some boundaries. I started to ask questions about the other person's language and behavior but stopped myself. The answer isn't found in deciphering and analyzing. This is presumptive and inaccurate. What's more important is tuning into how we feel around someone. Do I feel open? Do I feel excited? Do I feel like I have to censor myself or do I feel like I can share my thoughts as they come, imperfectly and enthusiastically?

Is there someone in your life you feel uneasy around? Direct this feeling inward. Where do you feel discomfort when you talk to them? Does it fit into a pattern you have of any past traumas or sensitivities? Is there a way to validate the way you feel? Write what comes to mind. Next time this feeling comes up, try locating it in your body and breathe into it. You have a wealth of intuition inside you, and no matter how long you've been disconnected from it, you can return to it. Let this wisdom guide you. Learn what clarity and safety feel like in your body. Collect data like a scientist. Step back from a relationship if you feel the need to and see how the space feels.

Notice who you feel safe giving time, attention, and energy to and let this information strengthen your relationship to yourself and the people you want to be in community with.

WHAT DO YOU WANT TO FEEL MORE OF?

It's rarely about the material thing we want—the job, the home, the lover, the friendship. We want the feeling that comes with change. With a new job, we hope to feel fulfilled and inspired. With a better home, we hope to feel safe and comfortable. With a lover, we hope to feel secure and cared for. With friendship, we hope to feel a sense of belonging.

But what if these feelings are already available? What if we can practice feeling good now, because happiness, satisfaction, and inspiration are always a part of us?

Think about situations in your past when you've felt good in your body. What were the catalysts for these emotions? What conditions helped you access these feelings?

Use the affirmations below as inspiration to create your own mood board or mind map of feelings you'd like to feel more of. Practice activating them as if you don't have to wait for permission from external factors. This gives your brain and body something to remember, so you can more easily recognize when experiences and opportunities line up with these feelings. Think of it as temporary time travel into the future.

I feel good. I feel competent and confident in myself—I enter situations knowing what to do and how to do it. I express how I feel without hesitation. It's easy to connect with people, and healthy boundaries come naturally to me. I know how to let go when I'm holding on too tightly. I feel hopeful, but I don't feel entitled to any specific outcome. I find inspiration wherever I am. I have fun spending time alone and with people I love. I listen to my intuition effortlessly. I feel sexy! I feel at home in my body! I'm so grateful for this romance, adventure, playfulness, and rest. It's so comforting to experience fulfilling companionship on a regular basis. I believe in myself. I'm not afraid to express how I feel. I love the company I keep. I feel safe. I trust myself completely.

● ●

WHEN YOUR FRIEND IS UNAVAILABLE

community care
does not mean
forgetting yourself

a reminder as every text I send
this morning sits without return

maybe this is not an antidote
maybe these are not my people

maybe I am reaching for the wrong medicine
maybe I'm not even sick

in *As We See It* (a show about 3 autistic people)
Violet's brother says something like
you'll find her endearing
until you find her annoying

so I am always waiting
for my sweetness
to be swallowed

this effort to connect
rarely reciprocated
(is this true?)

is it unhealthy
how available I am?

> the next time someone calls
> I wait a few seconds to answer
> just to show—I can be like everyone else

please send someone
with a similar capacity

if I stop talking to you
it's because I don't see a future for us

I share this fear with a friend
who says: *I dare you to annoy me*
I'm hard to annoy, I live to love
our friendship becomes a forest
sturdies through the year
both of us unafraid
to be available

but all of this waiting and reaching
and needing and searching teaches me:
I'm not needy for having needs
I can fulfill these needs through creative means
and I can be just as available to myself

EVEN DISAPPOINTMENT IS A SIGN THAT YOU CARE

People are disappointing. We just are. We forget to text each other back. We cancel at the last minute. We say we're going to do something and then we don't. We fail to say sorry and thank you. We get excited, form expectations, and let each other down.

I'm not afraid to admit that as a relatively mature adult, I still sometimes take it personally when my closest friends don't text me back quickly. I feel like a hurt puppy. Hello? Did you forget about me? Did I do okay the last time we hung out? I'm not getting enough validation—please feed me attention and words of encouragement!

I've learned through acute self-reflection that a lot of these feelings come from the fear that I am too traumatized to be loved. Growing up, I had to learn how to give myself advice because I couldn't rely on my family to be an emotional support system. Now, as I'm learning I can depend on others for some of that support, I can fall into an all-or-nothing mentality, and it can be hard to remember that people still love me even if they aren't always available.

This anxiety, and my autistic tendency to take words literally, have made for a cycle of expectations, disappointment, and turnover in my friendships. Maybe you're like this too. Maybe you're still developing a secure relationship with yourself and others. Maybe you send enthusiastic texts and get sad when they're not returned. Maybe you have a pattern of putting pressure on your friendships because you see your friends as your family.

These experiences are especially common for disabled and neurodivergent people. Our openness to connecting earnestly within extractive, shame-inducing cultures can be taken advantage of. It hurts to be pitied when we just want our honesty to be reciprocated. These feelings of disappointment don't always need to be reframed. It can be worse to suppress them, a way of gaslighting yourself when really, it's okay to want from people what you eagerly give.

It's okay to be romantic, to be sentimental, to be a big, brave lover with a rich capacity to feel. Know that even disappointment is a sign that you have the ability to care, that you want to connect, and that you deserve to be wanted and appreciated for everything you are.

COMPARE, DESPAIR

no history like yours
no body like yours
no longitude latitude
astrological placement
like yours

no desire like yours
no memory like yours
no losing, no searching
no grieving like yours

no precision like yours
no timeline like yours
no survival, no plot
no chronicle like yours

no vocabulary like yours
no method like yours
no one, no one
no one like yours

not directly, not exactly
not completely absolutely

no wonder
no wonder
no wonder
it's yours

CONVERTING THE ENERGY OF JEALOUSY AND ENVY

Let's face it. We compare ourselves to others. All the time. We gauge our career milestones, daily levels of productivity, family dynamics, quality of friendships, and lifestyles. No need to blame ourselves for this. We're taught a mentality of scarcity, that we must compete for finite resources. Jealousy and envy are something we all feel, no matter how mature or enlightened we become. We don't evolve out of our emotions, no matter how much we meditate or therapize or decolonize.

Engaging in new conversations about race, gender, and history might give you even more points of comparison that can activate new levels of anger, confusion, and resentment. These are growing pains as you develop your consciousness. Resentment can be redirected. Anger can be alchemized. Think of jealousy and envy as catalysts for growth, guiding you toward more compassionate perspectives.

When you notice yourself digging deeper into comparison, try writing out the fears behind the feeling of jealousy. *If I had a different upbringing, if I had more resources, if I had a partner, if I didn't have chronic pain, if I was more extroverted and had more connections, then maybe I could . . .*

Slow the thoughts down enough to look at them. Break down the logic. These comparisons are your brain's way of making sense of your experiences.

Racism, sexism, ableism, queerphobia, transphobia, classism, and all the other -isms maintain an inequitable status quo. It's valid to compare our traumas, and it's valid to resent the extra effort you've had to expend to "keep up" with those who have power and privilege. But it can be helpful to reframe these feelings. Identify any characteristics of creativity or empathy you've developed navigating a society not set up for your success.

What do you want to enact in your life so that the legacy you leave doesn't repeat the exhaustion, pain, or loneliness you've experienced? Imagine the childhood you wish you had and try to practice it for the generation that will come after you. Whether you have children or not, your legacy is in the impact you have on all the people you reach in your lifetime.

HONESTLY

As an autistic person and a first-generation American, I meticulously study the way people communicate. I take note of what people say and when, the tone and cadence of how they say it, and patterns in how people respond. I've noticed this: People don't always mean what they say or say what they mean.

Instead of saying, "I don't like this," or "This is making me jealous," it's more common for people to divert attention away from how they're really feeling. Many of us aren't taught how to be honest with ourselves. Many of us don't feel safe sharing how we're feeling because we're afraid that thinking "bad" thoughts makes us a "bad person." Embracing the complexities of who we are requires us to accept all of our multitudes—even the weird, unkind, and problematic parts.

Remember, unlearning white supremacy, ableism, and heteropatriarchy is a lifelong process. If you notice yourself thinking in a way that perpetuates harm, acknowledge it without punishing yourself.

I wonder what kind of conversations we could have if we were honest about these feelings that society teaches us are unlovable, that we're supposed to hide.

Practice saying something that feels hard to say. Admit a fear you've been holding in and see what it's like to accept where you are without letting it define who you are.

ASK FOR WHAT YOU REALLY WANT

Manifesting is a process of connecting to what we really want. How many of us have been taught that what we want is too ambitious, too improbable, too idealistic, too much?

We're taught to dream inside neat, linear boxes. *If it doesn't have immediate value, throw it away. If we can't be excellent, we might as well not try at all.* We dispose of thoughts and things because we have been taught to prioritize efficiency and normalcy over imagination and possibility.

But when we decide what we want in specific detail and are clear about our reasons for wanting it, we can move toward our dreams with intuitive guidance and the collective power of community. We aren't meant to fulfill our dreams alone.

Trust your excitement. Listen to your pleasures. Believe your passion. If it keeps coming back to you and points to something you've continuously cared about, it's connected to something larger than yourself.

When you dream with distinct intentions, you are contributing to collective liberation. Freeing yourself from the limitations you've been taught about your life is a way of reframing harmful narratives around worthiness, acceptance, and belonging. You deserve to ask the universe for what you really want.

THE COST OF SAFETY

April 13, 2022

a New Yorker
fires ten rounds
on the R train
headed north
I text two
friends who live
in sunset park
Are you safe?

the next day
I find myself
counting
nine more stops
eight more stops
seven more stops
until Spring Street

what choice
do we have
but to keep counting
calling a car
would cost
$38.66 and
I'm tired of paying
for this fear

this time I've
spent counting
I could have
spent living
like others do

WHAT DOES SAFETY FEEL LIKE TO YOU?

The past few years have activated a horrifying level of collective anxiety. As I write this in January 2023, there are reports of a mental health crisis among Asian Americans in response to the traumatic attacks spurred by xenophobic, racist rhetoric during the pandemic. With weekly mass shootings, a growing climate crisis, multiple viruses, and economic hardship, our sense of security is understandably shaky. Even with thought work, breathwork, meditation, and other mindfulness tools, it's hard to self-soothe our way out of collective trauma. A collective crisis requires collective strategy.

The murders of Christina Yuna Lee and Michelle Alyssa Go impacted my sense of safety as an Asian woman in New York City and made me hesitant to walk around outside alone. As I shared my fears, my friends reached out to offer rides home, a walking buddy to my next destination, and reminders that I have a community of people ready to support me. These offerings showed me that safety is a communal mission and something I don't have to create alone.

Think about a time in your life you felt safe. Who were you with? What were you doing? Where were you? Visualize this sense of safety and breathe into it. Remember this feeling the next time you feel anxious and let it be an anchor back into the present.

EVERY DAY A DIFFERENT DEATH

Put it in a letter. Don't send it, unless you must. Write to yourself too.

Do it differently. Do it yourself, your way.

Try gently. Stop when you need to.

Proceed into the past as slowly as you need.

Note what did/didn't feel okay.

Remember this next time someone says,
let me know if you need anything.

Change the story's shape. Shift seats. Ask for another perspective.

Walk away. Toward something that will hold this era of you.

Keep one secret a day to yourself. Just to remember you can.

Phone a friend.

Wish them well even if they don't answer.

Ask imperfectly.

Play a song on shuffle. Make a melody out of the misery.

Accept every part as a whole. Even the emptiness.

Make daily appointments with the child in you who wants to play.

Share something without expecting it to return.

Let the release be a part of the giving.

Grieve what you realize you never had.

Mine your history for the most generous interpretation.

Listen to your intuition if it says "go no further"
without probing for explanations.

Remember, history changes with the view.

When you need to pause before a decision, say, *I need a minute.*

For goodness sake, *JUST SAY IT!*

Be an observer. There is less saving needed than you think.

Daydream out loud with someone you love.

Breathe like a bath.

Memorize this safety.

Enjoy now. Save the excess.

Let boredom be a border. Pivot to a different destination.

Decide when the time comes.

Collaborate with change.

Abolish with patience. For your own sake.

Believe you know enough to continue learning.

Connect the dots later.

Disappear, if you need. Return with reminders.

Pace the progress—not all at once!

If the nightmares wake you up, breathe in/out/in/out.

Exhale until the terror leaves you.

Too much healing, and your body
will think the wound is bigger than it is.

Don't write with an empty pen.

The tenth time you feel the void, try filling it with
something other than cannabis and/or company.

If stuck, put into motion the one body part that will move.

When on fire, stay away from bridges.

When cringing, know that no one remembers the way you do.

When you feel like you're at an end, fall into its depth.

Let each end deepen you.

Remember, you are your own roots.

Remember, this dying is a form of living, too.

Change is a calling and creative practice.

> — *Alice Wong, founder and director of the Disability Visibility Project, during a speech for the Autistic Self Advocacy Network Gala in November 2019*

THIS DIFFERENCE

As I started changing elements of my life in response to the
pandemic and healing from the impact of systemic oppression,
I found myself asking different questions. Do I really want this,
or do I want this because others do? What other options do
I have? As I practiced expanding my imagination, my beliefs
around gender, friendship, labor, and love expanded too. Turn
to this section when you're moving through a fundamental
shift in your life, when you know you want something different
but you're in the in-between before somewhere new.

BECOMING NONBINARY

the more I realize
gender is a performance

the more I want to
write my own role

the more I see how complex it is
the more I want to have a say
in its complexity

my pronouns are they/them
because I believe
feminine, masculine
can be accessed by all
because I am changing
every day and shouldn't
my gender expression be
as fluid as the rest of me
because only I know
how I feel when I hear
them because gender is
not just about presentation,
it's about choices, sensations,
inner ecosystems because
pronouns are a way of shaping
our language, language as a
way of shaping perception
and if we can challenge our
binary language, we can challenge
all binary forms of thinking, believing,
and existing . . . and because I believe
in transcending binary ways of being

UNDOING THE PERFORMANCE OF GENDER

For most of my life, I thought of gender as something fixed within a binary—either feminine or masculine. This belief defined every aspect of my life from how I loved to how I ached. Because of this body I was born into and the ways I'm perceived, I bought into the idea that I had to perform the part of a "girl."

Being a girl in a strict, conservative, Southern, Christian, immigrant household came with rules and expectations. Women are in service to men. Women are caretakers. Women quietly suffer while men get to rage without consequence. I resisted this dynamic, but no one in my world was modeling an alternative.

The #MeToo movement gave me language and frameworks to pull apart the gendered power dynamics that had negatively influenced my life. At the same time, I noticed how much safer and freer I felt in queer social spaces and within the company of queer friends. I started to openly identify as queer and sharpened my political values by learning from queer and trans thought leaders.

The protests against police violence during the summer of 2020 created a cultural shift, and the isolation of the pandemic relieved many of us from the pressure of performing for others. I started committing to a practice of decolonization, and to decolonize it felt necessary to divest from all binary forms of thinking and embrace a more fluid identity. The gender binary didn't make sense to me anymore. I wanted something different—I wanted the choice to embrace both femininity and masculinity while opting out of the idea that I had to fit into normative expressions of either.

Gender is something I'm in ongoing, shifting relationship with. I identify with the politics of being a woman in many ways since this is how I've lived most of my life, but being queer means constantly questioning the limits that have been projected onto me. This, to me, is a process of freeing myself. By believing in self-determination, agency, and abundance, I understand that there are as many expressions of gender as there are people. This also helps me remember that people are more complex than how we perceive them. I am nonbinary, genderfluid, and queer because I believe in a future where everyone has the support they need to feel safe as they are. I am nonbinary because I believe in a future where everyone is free.

EMBRACING DUALITY

so much grief I want it all gone

so much joy I want to hold it all

MAYBE FEELING ONE

there isn't enough

there's more than enough

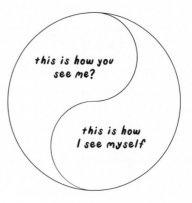

this is how you see me?

this is how I see myself

HELPS FREE THE OTHER

what I believed yesterday

what I'll believe tomorrow

QUEERING COMPANY

it's difficult
to tell you
I feel uneasy
not because
I don't love you
but because lately
I have been wanting to
love more of myself
the me I have hidden
the me I have tamed for 30 years
three decades is
a long time to undo   to remake

when I am in queer spaces
I feel I must prove
my queerness
if I speak of my
attraction for one
gender expression
I feel I must also speak of
other gender expressions
to prove that I belong
that my desires bend past
cisheteronormative boundaries
that I too speak the
language of the future

but this bending
this stretching
feels like it expands me

more than it contracts me
challenges me to
taste my own desires

what is the friend equivalent
of *it's not you*
because it really is me
it is me— the way I want to
wrap myself in queerness
like a shield, like armor
like an embellished jumpsuit

here's a theory:
<u>everyone is queer</u>
<u>they just don't know it yet</u>
everyone is queer
but not all have challenged
the norms they've been molded into
and reimagined what pleasure can
look like when it comes from within
when expressed without rules
without fear of exclusion and censorship

it doesn't feel fair to have only
one archetype of romance for the rest
of your life   *your life deserves more romance than this!*

maybe to be queer
is to look from a
different angle
and maybe most of us
are terrified of heights

maybe to be queer
is to be in resistance
and maybe most of us
are tired, muscles aching
from all this living

maybe to be queer
is to want inside a wondering
maybe once I began
asking different questions
the theory of heteronormativity
became unbearably boring

maybe it's because
our lives reflect our fears
and once I began
cracking myself out of

the shell that kept me secretive
about my bisexuality
drove me away from
the word pansexual
pan, bi, demi, sexual
thinking sex was
all there is to sexuality

I stopped knowing how
to fit into your shell

because that's what two people
in conversation are
two shells chipping away
at ourselves, at each other

two shells getting to know
each other's shape
feeding off each
other's language
shapeshifting
toward each other

and this is not to say
my non-queer
(again, the ones who have yet
to realize their queerness)
friends have unacceptable shells
this is not to say
they are not worthy
of care and attention
and this is not to say
I no longer see the value
in their company

this is simply to say
I am queering my company

What are our choices as we think about journeys to sexual freedom? . . . I think of Tim Dean's work on being queer—queer as not about who you're having sex with, that can be a dimension of it, but queer as being about the self that is at odds with everything around it and has to invent and create and find a place to speak and to thrive and to live.

> — *bell hooks, referencing the work of scholar Tim Dean on a panel at The New School in 2014 titled, "Are You Still a Slave? Liberating the Black Female Body"*

GRIEVING FRIENDSHIPS

As you grow and change, so do your values. You develop an awareness of harm and abuse and the vocabulary to call things as you see them. This is you learning how to challenge long-held beliefs. Because you're evolving, you might lose friends who aren't on a similar journey of liberating themselves. Not everyone is healing from the stories racism, sexism, ableism, and queerphobia have taught them. This doesn't make them bad people, but it might make them incompatible with you in this season of your life.

Let your community change with you. You have a right to be in relationship with people who have shared values and interests. Abolition teaches us that people are not disposable and transformative justice principles help us move through conflict with each other. At the same time, you're not obligated to stay in a friendship with someone just because you have history with them.

Write about any friendships you've lost over the past few years. Are there themes across the conflicts you've been a part of? What did you learn about yourself through these experiences? What do you bond over in your current relationships? Do you feel like care and mutual respect are actively practiced with the people in your life?

VISUALIZATION TO LET GO OF WHATEVER YOU'RE HOLDING ON TO

Imagine yourself as a cloud. Take a moment to really imagine the sensory experience of this—how your body would feel if it were fluffy, floating in the sky.

Envision yourself sinking into a warm color, like burnt orange or golden yellow. Breathe as deeply as you can and feel your chest rise and fall, each breath softening your edges. You are not the same as you were one, two, three breaths ago. You are always in motion. You are always changing.

A child is looking up at the sky and points to you—hey, cool cloud! You receive the compliment and smile because yes, you are a very cool cloud.

Another cloud is wrapping its arms around you like a blanket. Soft, so soft. Let your body melt into this feeling. Say thanks to this cloud, then keep it moving.

Now, imagine yourself soaring through the sky. The sky is infinite, expansive, stretches beyond the horizons of what you can see. Feel the wind supporting you. Move as fast or as slow as you want. Up, down, left, right, diagonally, in loops. Let your intuition direct you.

With this momentum, move into a different area of the sky. Once you're there, take a few deep breaths. Notice how it feels here.

When you're done, record this feeling in your memory. Bookmark this experience for the next time you feel stuck or stressed. Use this technique to release whatever you're holding that isn't yours to hold and return back to a sense of relaxation and clarity. This visual is a reminder that you're always changing, and you're allowed to shift, move positions, and be fluid in how you show up.

Let this feeling carry you through the rest of your day.

● ●

A DIFFERENT QUESTION, PLEASE

in a dream, I'm in the
passenger seat of a
friend's car as I ask
how are you?

they stop me

> *no—no more pretending*
> *we're not going to perform this script*
> *written for when we're afraid to speak*
> *from the heart, we're going to stop this game*
> *ask different questions*

> > sometimes I feel like conversations
> > are trains going in the wrong direction
> > too heavy to turn, to stop, to stand in front of
> > so I let it run its course, knowing it's headed
> > towards a cliff, an ending, anticipating the drop
> > in my mind I yell *please stop! I don't like this!*
> > *this doesn't feel good!*

but I don't say anything
because I don't know
how to interject
without being rude
without damaging
the moment
without derailing
the entire friendship

I don't know how to
dance a tango
I've only practiced dancing
with my own two feet

    what if we   each other
       slow danced   next to
      with our   selves

what if I stopped
hopscotching between
        is this me
        is this you
        the programming
        the social norms
        the power plays
        the performance
        the people pleasing
        the trauma responses

what if we can have a
different conversation
if we both let go of the wheel

SOCIAL CURRENCY

There is a cost to this conversation.
I feel it as I'm in it. This tangling, this timing.
There is no speaking with, only speaking to.

There is a cost to this conversation
and I did not budget for a purchase.
I came to sit. Body next to body,
sounds slicing through these speakers
spilling across all this vocal traffic.

I came here to chew. You are throwing
things into my belly, quicker than I can taste.
There is no savoring here.

There is a cost to this conversation
and I'm sinking before the main course.

I shouldn't have come, I could have listened
to the signs that warned: do not proceed.
Sometimes, I don't know if this voice comes
from care or fear. Careful fear, fearful care.
Sometimes I listen, only sometimes.

The lesson here: you do not have to be friends
with everyone who wants to be friends with you.
You are allowed to choose.

There is a cost to this conversation and
sure I wouldn't be here if I counted my
spoons* before I came but we are here
and you are talking like hail like snow
and your posture is telling me you're

very invested and I am looking at
your left my right eyeball to stay
in my seat because I read on reddit,
something scientific about brain
pathway connection. It said, watch
like an eye of a hurricane.
Let the storm pass.

So I hold my breath because
that is what you do when you are
holding your tongue and I tell myself:
This is not terror. This is discernment.

There is a cost to this conversation
and I know I'll be paying it later
so I think of water like rain,
like shower, like bath,
and I think of what I'm
learning in acting class,
about saying how I really feel
no matter the cost and I'm not that
rich yet so I smile like I'm shy
and I count to goodbye and I tell myself
I'm so proud of you for making it outside.

There is a cost to this conversation
and maybe one day I'll tell you why.

* The spoon theory was coined by writer and blogger Christine Miserandino in 2003 to
describe the fatigue she feels while living with chronic illness. It has since been used by
disabled people to describe what it's like to have a limited amount of energy while moving
through the physical, mental, and social demands of everyday life.

CONVERSATION AS A BALANCING ACT

I am autistic. I don't have much of an information hierarchy, so I tend to either ignore or challenge expressions of power that perpetuate inequity. I can hear about someone's childhood trauma as if I were receiving just another piece of information, like what they did this morning or their favorite food—all data points to understand who they are. Even so, there's still a somatic impact to sharing intimate details about our lives with each other. Though I don't like to subscribe to the idea of "too much, too soon," thinking about an interpersonal exchange as a balancing act helps me understand when one person is taking up space in a way that another person might not have the capacity for. Talking about trauma can activate trauma in ourselves and others, and there should be a practice of care within conversations to invite active presence and psychological safety. This helps us process information reciprocally instead of creating a dynamic where one person is taking on more emotional weight without wanting to.

Capacity changes day to day, even second to second. We might feel okay during the start of a conversation and then have a change of heart a moment later. Approaching conversations with mutual consent gives us permission to change our boundaries as we learn more information. Think of consent as giving permission to your intuition. This helps us sustain the practice of intimacy.

To avoid emotional dumping or emotional violations, try checking in before sharing.

Hey, do you have capacity to talk about this?

What's your headspace like right now? Can you talk?

I'm having trouble with _____. Are you comfortable talking through it with me?

I need to vent. Are you in a place to listen?

I want to share something about _____. Is that okay or should I wait for a different time?

Can I share a thought about _____ with you?

Are you comfortable talking about _____?

• •

THERE ARE NO MORAL BINARIES

people are neither inherently
good nor inherently bad
they are put in situations
circumstances that bring out
their good, their bad

like the mud monster
in *Spirited Away*
scary until he soaks
the mud away

like the no-face spirit
when Chihiro says
I think the bathhouse
makes him crazy
he ate the people
not because he was a monster
but because the bathhouse
brought the monster out of him

maybe we all have a monster in us
maybe the monster rages
when we're twisted into answering
the same questions over and over
extracting the same explanations
again and again

maybe there is a lover in all of us
maybe the lover comes out to play

when given encouragement
safety, space, patience, support

                                      like this saying
if you judge a fish
by how well it can
climb a tree
it will go its whole life
thinking it is dumb

I have felt like that fish
in creative reviews
this thing they do at
advertising agencies where
you come up with ideas and
white men in khaki shorts
accustomed to authority
pull it apart and crush your vision

                                  as one of few
(femme, Asian, neurodivergent)
in the creative department
the tree was the pace
the tree was the game
of how well I could speak
bro talk
(I am 0% fluent in bro talk, dude)
how well I could get along
how well I could pretend

I was a floundering fish
and thought, I am a terrible writer
because I cannot climb
this damn tree

because I am always
100 steps behind
watching from below
and even as I watched
I thought
I don't want this
I don't want to be in this tree
why am I trying to climb in this direction
why don't I plant my own forest
feel into the shape of my own trunk
tune into the wisdom of my own roots

I became a monster
because I did not belong
in that bathhouse
so maybe
none of us are monsters
maybe all of us can become monsters

maybe all of us can be
fish swimming free
if we're put in a stream
instead of a damn tree

LITERARY RELIEF

i don't drink alcohol
so i sip poetry
like a tonic
this way
to shape the sorry
to feed the wanting
to lead the lonely

i get drunk off memories
and stumble through time
backwards, forwards

i don't drink alcohol
so i let these words
loosen me instead

i turn pages till i'm tipsy
until enough time passes
for me to say
i'm no longer
living in this story

DECOLONIZING YOUR LIBRARY

The films, books, music, and art we interact with confirm and challenge our beliefs. Be intentional about where you source your information. Look for stories outside the margins of what you know, voices you haven't learned from before. If there are people, words, or references in this book that aren't familiar to you, write them down to look through later. Decolonizing is a practice of broadening your knowledge of history, thinking with more nuance, and understanding the roots of systemic oppression. This inevitably shapes the way you experience the world around you. Keep an intentionally curated library of knowledge, knowing this is the information that informs the direction in which you grow.

DIASPORIC DEBT

my mother, after a twenty-minute setup
   asks for twenty thousand dollars

your stepfather was fired, he blew a whistle
   got cut for causing trouble
      he's been depressed
   working weekends
but it's going to get better
   we just need twenty thousand dollars
      for a new venture

my mother asks me for twenty thousand dollars
calls back twenty minutes later
   I don't need it anymore
   never mind, we'll figure it out
      I'm sorry to bother you
         we'll figure it out, we always do

      you are my daughter, I'm not supposed to ask you
   to this I think, *you are my mother*
      there was a lot of supposed tos that we didn't do
   and this is what happens when you come from
      a lineage of women who built sanctuaries in everyone
                                             except themselves

so I invest six thousand into a life coach / three thousand into psychedelic
therapy / hundreds a month in psychotherapy / somatic coaching /
workshops and webinars to understand trauma / to understand my
history / to find a different future / to medicate my memories

the next time someone
asks me what my rate is

I want to tell them

this is the lineage of debt I'm paying for

I'M STILL HEALING

I'm still healing from the idea that I'm not
big enough, good enough for the life I want
I'm still healing from the lie that I am unlovable
too much to love, too complex to learn

from the idea that there can only be one
and more than that is too much, the world cannot handle
two of something if they're too similar to each other

from the idea that intimacy and romance
only exist with sex, only exist between a m/f binary

from the idea that I'm not worthy of love
without offering something of extra, profound value

from the idea that I have to hate myself
when I don't match my expectations of
what a good person is
that I must push and punish into higher standards

from the feeling of being alone, of feeling unknown
of being left behind, of not keeping up,
of being embarrassed of success

I'm still healing

from the idea that I have to do it alone
that there's no one who can commit to holding my hand
from the idea that I don't know how to hold myself

from the impulse to return what (and when) I receive

from the idea that I have to give
    until I'm empty before saving some for myself

        from the idea that I have to share everything
            as soon as I think it because what if it floats away

                from the idea that I'm wrong for thinking
                    ugly thoughts, selfish thoughts,
                    judgmental thoughts
                        that I can instead love myself through it
                            that instead I can meet myself with
                                okay, I'm here and that's okay

        thank this too, send love to this part too

        and though I'm urgent in the beauty of
        making things meaningful

    be easy on me, I'm still healing

WHAT ARE YOU HEALING FROM?

What limiting beliefs do you find yourself reverting back to?

Do you believe you can change? Why or why not?

What do you want more of from the people around you?

What do you want more of from yourself?

What lies have white supremacy, patriarchy, heteronormativity, ableism, and capitalism taught you?

What would you rather believe?

THIS IS MY VERSION OF FLYING

on Thursday, I allowed myself to be free   like a bird
I flew with the direction of the pack
let the wind take me where it willed
Thursday, I flew
twelve queer friends
humming through Central Park
staggered, like a parade
a soft chorus of safety

within an hour
I'm over!stimulated
my body receiving
too much information
to compute at once

loud speakers, many mouths
different stories, too many sounds
rain, falling falling
dodging drops on skin
this makeup too precise to get wet
sit, stand, squish
no one knows where we're going
but together, at least we are together

I move with the pack
I allow myself to be a bird

careful in this crowd
    delta variant, new strains
        bare-faced risks, because we are tired
            because we want to see each other

                after a year apart
                    to touch each another
                        see our mouths moving
                            we've been missing out on these memories
                            so much to catch up on,
                            so many stories to make up for

    I am conflicted. Are we considering the impact of this pandemic?

a friend says
we are many selves at once
this, a source of our madness
the source of our brilliance too, I'm sure
the child we were is still a part of us
and sometimes they scream
IS THIS REALLY HAPPENING
WE DIDN'T THINK
THIS WOULD REALLY HAPPEN

so we have to
talk to ourselves
like a child

loosen the grip
let go of the grasp
let yourself be
in conversation with
these THESE people
we're here
dressed in
calvin klein

we're here
beautiful, sexy bodies
as Ocean Vuong says,
we're only briefly gorgeous

we might as well have a ball with this brevity

queer bodies
    beautiful bodies, queered
        we're here
            they're dreamers
                just like you
                    you're a dreamer
                        just like them

in this dream, we can hold each other

I wonder if this is the chapter
where my dream gets bigger

I mean really,
what do you do
how do you continue
when your dreams
are right in front of you

I learn: I can't take a compliment
I think: everyone is lying to me

it makes me uneasy
to be admired

don't look up at me
I'm too close to falling

I forget I am doing things
    things?: writing, modeling, speaking, sharing, learning, reading,
    studying, showing up, healing, feeling, growing, paving, pivoting

I committed to this
I didn't know what I'd do
I didn't plan for the part
when the success becomes real

I didn't do it for this
it feels wrong
to receive praise
for something I channeled
as if I'm taking credit for god
    yes, I know god is within me
        I see this is hard to understand

is it real? did it happen? will it last?
Octavia Butler: *all that you touch you change*
all that you change changes you
the only lasting truth is change

I am changed.
my shape is new.
I am still confused.

how do you come down from the high
    when you're flying
    with friends
    FLYING! and I mean flying
    with friends
    and they remain in flight

my body, too heavy to do more than breathing
    and this, I'm barely doing
I see, for most
there is no recovery time
they can move on
I see, for me
    I am forced into recovery
where I slip into
why me, why can't I move on like them

                        this feels like I'm being left behind

perhaps
and I really mean
just perhaps
as I'm in bed
resting // lights off // mouth dry // stomach empty // spirit gone
temporarily
synthesizing
metabolizing
integrating
returning

                              perhaps

THIS IS MY VERSION OF FLYING

FOR WHEN YOU FEEL TOO DAMAGED TO BE LOVED

As you grieve former versions of yourself and grow into the next season of you, your inner critic might try to keep you from the love and care you deserve. It can be hard finding new friends and building a different community, and it's okay to be resistant to this work. Your brain might tell you lies like: you're too damaged, you've done too much harm to others, you're doing too little too late. Remember: This impossible standard of perfection is rooted in racism, patriarchy, and ableism. No one is unlovable. One of the principles of abolition and transformative justice is that everyone is redeemable. Instead of thinking of care as something we have to earn, we can be fierce in our belief that we can meet love from wherever we are.

Use these affirmations to change the way you relate to yourself. Write them over and over again. Record a voice note and share with a friend. Incorporate them into an illustration, giving them distinct shapes and colors. Write them on sticky notes and stick them to your mirror. Know that even if the words don't sink in immediately, the kindness you're practicing is building a muscle of self-compassion that you can use as a resource for the next time you feel unlovable. Write down any other affirming truths that come to mind.

Love still exists even when it's not expressed.

I love and accept all of me, now.

I'm growing and healing even if I don't feel the progress today.

Love is always possible for me.

My love is limitless.

This discomfort is a part of my growth.

Everything I've done and everywhere I've been has prepared me for the life I want to live.

Anything can change in an instant.

I have endured so much. I'm so proud of me.

I'm lovable for who I am, not what I can do.

• •

TRYING NEW ROUTES

I've spent years living in New York City, and I still lose my way. I sometimes get on the wrong train going the wrong direction, and every trip through a subway station makes me feel like a frazzled character in a video game. My sense of spatial awareness and ability to discern between north, south, east, and west has never been a strength.

When I look up my commute with a navigation app, it computes the most direct and available route. But this doesn't consider the noisiness or safety of a road, the time of day, if I'm alone or with someone, or my current capacity. My route then becomes something I determine with the factors I can't input into a machine. I must rely on my intuition.

A therapist explained neuroplasticity to me by saying the brain is like an ice-skating rink. The more we think certain thoughts and practice certain habits, the more we deepen the grooves. Each time we redirect ourselves from shame and criticism to love and acceptance, the route becomes smoother. This is how we reshape our brain to think more compassionately.

With this in mind, try leaving thirty minutes early the next time you go to a familiar place and let yourself get lost. Notice new landmarks, trees, or gardens along the way. Is there a way you can apply this practice of finding a new perspective to the way you talk to yourself, the way you talk to others? Is there different ground you can cover, a different opening for different dialogue? A change of pace and scenery can help jump-start a new habit. Consider this a way of building a new groove.

WHAT IS DIFFERENT ABOUT THESE SHAPES?

people who want
to be friends with me

me

people I want to
be friends with

will we ever meet?
what space will we make?

will you love the way I need to be loved?
will I love the way you want to be needed?

can you hold this shape of me?
can I hold this shape of you?

in spiritual communities, they say
everyone is a teacher

will you learn my language?
will you show me how to learn yours?

will you wait for me?

what will we share?
what will we swallow?

will you want me beyond convenience?

will you bring out my honesty?
can you hold my truth?

every word in a conversation, a shape
this is why we must leave space

to calibrate

WHAT IF IT'S NOT ABOUT YOU?

Sometimes I think about people as shooting stars—everyone moving on their own trajectory across a spacious galaxy. I imagine balls of light, sparking up, fizzling out, pulled into various orbits. Sometimes we move harmoniously alongside each other and sometimes we collide and conflict. Sometimes we even disappear, without warning or reason. Thinking of someone as having a unique path in life helps me avoid dwelling on my pain when I feel hurt or disappointed. It's fruitless to make assumptions when I don't have the full view of the galaxy.

Relationships of every kind require labor to maintain. The effort we make to nurture a connection isn't always reciprocated. We won't always understand the mystery of why someone has stopped interacting with us. Sometimes people have incompatible chemistry, and sometimes relationships are temporary.

We are balls of light with feelings, constantly adjusting to and influencing the atmosphere around us. It's helpful to remember: It's not you; it's the nature of a complex, mystifying galaxy.

SELF-TALK

I want to follow every conversation with

did I do okay?

did I do okay?

did I do okay?

did I do okay?

did I do okay?

did I do okay?

did I do okay?

did I do okay?

did I do okay?

did I do okay?

MEDITATION FOR SOCIAL ANXIETY

When you are afraid of saying or doing the wrong thing:

Probably, this person is also thinking a version of what you're thinking.

Probably, this is a normal part of interacting with other people.

Probably, this connection is worth the effort.

Return to the room.

Feel your body in this seat. Feel the temperature of where you are.

Feel the clothes on your skin. Feel your chest rise and fall.

Slow breaths, even slower. Quiet the thoughts, sit with them longer.

It's okay to be awkward. It's okay to be weird.

This experience is what makes you interesting.

Honestly, it's what makes you alive.

FOR THE PEOPLE PLEASERS

People pleasing is not inherently bad. At the heart of this habit is a desire to love and be loved. It's a practice of compassion and connection. It's when this habit goes into overdrive, when we disconnect from our needs, that it becomes unsustainable and potentially harmful.

Before practicing somatics, I was so used to *yes* that I forgot I could say *no*. As an Asian woman and a child of immigrants, I've been conditioned to go above and beyond expectations and be agreeable by default. Through working with healing practitioners, I noticed the shape I take when I subconsciously submit to someone else's energy. I lean forward, I nod impulsively, furrow my brows, and hunch my shoulders.

Once I became aware of this physical posture, I realized that I sometimes literally bow to white people. Historical power dynamics are hard to shift. We can't just shift them intellectually, we also have to shift them within our body. Healing can then involve a process of changing the physical shapes we make.

A yes to me feels like a warm summer sun, like an open field, like the calm of an empty road. Physically, I tend to sway from side to side, my chin parallel to the ground, brows and eyes relaxed, shoulders pushed back. With an enthusiastic yes, I feel a warmth from my pelvis to my heart, like a blooming flower. There is no rush, no urgency.

A no feels like a winter shiver, like a tremor in my body, and I contract like something wilting. I feel small—my parameters shrink and my belly folds into my lap.

When I feel somewhere in between, that's a sign to ask for more time—to say I need a moment, I'm not sure yet, let me get back to you. I need more information or more space to understand what my body is saying.

Participating in a course called "Decolonizing the Body" by somatic practitioner Kelsey Blackwell helped me develop the language to locate the yes, no, and maybe in my body. Think back to a recent memory when you took on the shape of a pleaser—who were you talking to, what were the power dynamics, and how did you feel after? Bringing awareness to when and how our people-pleasing tendencies are activated can gently guide us back into our bodies and reconnect us to our power.

HOW TO SAY NO

Saying no can be hard if you've spent a lifetime saying yes. Feelings of scarcity, fear, and doubt are manifestations of urgency. *What if they don't invite me next time? What if I'm missing out on something that could change my life? Maybe I'm not as qualified as I thought?*

Saying no to something you don't want is a way of saying yes to what you value. You're allowed to change your mind. No single gig or job or assignment or relationship defines your future. And if you say yes when you meant to say no, there's learning in the experience. No one is a perfect communicator. We adapt and grow as we collect more information.

Write down some variations of "no" for both professional and interpersonal interactions. The next time someone requests something from you that you don't want to give, or the next time someone invites you to something you don't want to go to, return to these scripts. Prepare scripts to communicate boundaries now, so you can more easily access the language when the time comes. Here are some starters:

Thanks for thinking of me! I'm at capacity, so I'm going to pass.

This isn't speaking to me, so I'll step aside for a more fitting collaborator.

I'm so glad you're doing this. It sounds like a good time. I can't make it, but send me photos if you remember!

What a special opportunity. I'm focused on some other priorities, so I can't commit. I hope it goes well and you get exactly what you need.

THE GREAT ESCAPE

you're falling, but you're not in danger
you're falling, but you're not in danger
you're falling, but you're not in danger

I tell myself this
I rinse it around my mouth
learning its taste
I want to memorize
what it's like to trust myself

sometimes *yes* spills out of me
I see, my yes comes from
my need to be loved
I see, my fear of no
is a fear of being unlovable

you're falling and you're in danger
you're falling and you're in danger
you're falling and you're in danger

swish this danger around your mouth
become familiar with the feeling

no, this doesn't make you a bad person
yes, this makes the bad in you something to befriend

what if bad is also a spectrum
an exploration of potential

what do the Buddhist teachings say . . .
detach—stop the calculation
detach—let it leave you, the sense that you're

good or you're bad or you're right or you're wrong
detach—you are the ground, the sky
the thoughts are merely weeds to pull,
wind and rain to weather

breathe in from the belly
begin again, sprout new roots
believe there's a route you've yet to discover
find excitement for this expedition

fall into the hope and let it hold you

you're falling, and this is part of the freeing
you're falling, and there is no need to escape
you're falling, and the danger is coming from you

NAME IT

I am always spilling
    over
       over
          over

           how do you create a ritual
                around your unraveling?

               how do you pause
           how do you still
        how are you still here

    I am making amends
in advance

    I am terrified
  in advance

        I am grieving
      in advance

      what if I feel more alive
          when I'm swimming in my past

        what if I feel more alive in anticipation

      I cannot keep a secret
    about myself

   and I want to learn
 how to cry in public

this is where I am
what does this stillness have to say?

CARE COMPASS

Learning about the neurodiversity paradigm has helped me personalize my practice of self-care. Self-care that works for a neuronormative person might not work for me. Sometimes it feels like I have a sloth and a bunny living inside me—the sloth is my need for slowness and ease, and the bunny is my need for variety and adventure. The sloth and bunny show up in different ways, every day.

Using the following example, create your own self-care plan that considers the dimensionality of your sensory needs. Even if you don't identify as neurodivergent, creating a cheat sheet of things you can do to increase comfort in your life is helpful for when you feel overwhelmed, burned out, or lonely. Try laying it out in different shapes or write it on colorful pieces of paper—get creative and make it something you'll enjoy taping to your wall and looking at every day.

If you have a therapist or supportive friend group, share this list with them and let them know this is how you intend to care for yourself in this chapter of your life.

MY CARE COMPASS WHILE WRITING THIS BOOK

inspired by a series of questions from my therapist

Main intention: enjoy the process!

I want to feel: at ease, present, embodied, confident

I don't want to fall into: stress, self-doubt, disassociation, scarcity mindset

Signs to activate self-care: worrying, comparison, defeat, perfectionism, rumination, indecision, paralysis

Self-soothing: nap, self-massage, easy breathwork, put the phone down, write a letter to myself, stretch, sing a song, qi gong, read a page in a book, dance break, look through an old journal

If this doesn't work, call: Kimberly, Yanni, Chella, Sarah

Physical places for support: any large tree, playground or park, watch clouds from the couch

Comfort scents: lavender, eucalyptus, peppermint

Comfort sounds: *Funny Girl* soundtrack, *The Parent Trap* soundtrack, Beyoncé's *Homecoming: The Live Album*, Kiana Ledé's *Kiki*, SZA's *Ctrl*, Ariana Grande's *Sweetener*, Blonde piano tribute to Frank Ocean, lo-fi beats, Fold's *Aphelion: A Tribute to Lorraine Hansberry*, healing frequencies

Textures: plushies, stickers, hoodie, hot tea, pistachios, soft blanket

Boundaries: spend less time with people who don't help me feel safe/possible/inspired, be intentional about what is influencing my creativity, time limits on Instagram and TikTok

DIFFERENT PEOPLE

Different people, different memories.
Different people, different histories.
Different people, different lineage.
Different people, different language.
Different people, different taste.
Different people, different thoughts.
Different people, different boundaries.
Different people, different views.
Different people, different sounds.
Different people, different families.
Different people, different wounds.
Different people, different remedies.
Different people, different rhythms.
Different people, different bodies.
Different people, different grief.
Different people, different greed.
Different people. Different needs.

TRUST ME, I'VE TRIED IT

After thorough rounds of experimentation, I've reached the following conclusions: **wanting someone** to love you won't make them love you because wanting someone **doesn't mean** they'll want you back. When something doesn't feel right but **we** have a hard time explaining it, intuition is pointing us to something we **should** be listening to. It's hard to anticipate **stop** signs when it comes from the driver. The danger in **wanting** someone is that sometimes it keeps us from wanting **ourselves.**

THE STAMINA OF STORYTELLING

you have to get through the void
well, you don't have to
no hand is forcing you
no force is making you
but if you want this,
the tunnel is a part of the ride

this is where the story is
most think it happens at the beginning
ends at the end, but stories, like time
don't have distinct beginnings and endings
they fall asleep
they jolt you awake
in the middle of the night
they disappear, reappear
when you're eating pho
with a friend and someone
who broke your heart when
you were 22 walks by with
a kid they made in a life after you
except it's not them
it was an illusion

stories are illusions of our own making
we are our most reliable / unreliable narrators
reliability, responsibility
the truth requires these directives
and when you're alone at a desk or

scribbling memories into a notebook
the only thing reliable is your ability to write
so maybe the responsibility is in the doing
not the truth, just the digging

how was your day, a friend asks

I went through the void, I tell them

some people help the honesty spill out sooner

I tell my friend, the void was where I
drew circles across my memories
where I examined them with both hands
not with a twisted grip, but a gentle hold
a rocking, a swaying, a hand that stays
patient, curious

is that what really happened?
what else was happening at the time
that may have colored my interpretation?
who is the villain here, and does the villain
change depending on where I look?
does the story change if we make everyone
their own hero, everyone their own villain?

questions, the void requires questions
requires you to yell into nothingness
until you realize, there is no one there
to tell you how to feel
you choose the feelings
you choose the adventure

this is the terror
the magic of the void
you are the magician
you are the audience
you are the question

it takes all this to realize
you were writing the script all along

THE ART OF AFFIRMATIONS

I thrive with consistent and specific feedback. But because I can't always get this from other people, I've become skillful at sourcing comfort from myself. This practice also helps me better affirm others. It helps show people: This is how I like to be spoken to. The key with affirmations is specificity. Sometimes, "I miss you" or "I'm thinking of you" can still do the job, but colloquial sayings don't land with the same spirit as something tailored to the person you love. As an autistic person, sometimes these familiar phrases don't register with me because I'm not sure if someone really means what they're saying or if it's a social script without much intention (sometimes it can be both). Clear and direct descriptions about my impact help me feel validated in my unique experience.

Using the next few poems as inspiration, write down some specific words of affirmation for the people in your life. Or imagine writing a love note to yourself and apply the same level of specificity.

I FEEL FOR YOU

I feel water for you.
I feel ocean for you.
I feel wind and sky
full airbender for you.
I feel motion for you.
I feel garden for you.
I feel trees waving hi!
outside my window for you.
I feel leaves for you.
I feel weakened knees for you.
I feel blue and green and
eyes all googly for you.
I feel depth for you.
I feel rain for you.
Have I told you?
I feel the weather get
warmer in my chest with you.
I feel weight for you.
I feel wonder for you.
I feel like swimming in
the summertime air for you.
I feel seasons for you.
I feel safety for you.
I feel blanket wrapped around
all my width for you.
I feel mad for you.
I feel sad for you.

I'm learning how to feel on my own for you.
I promise you
I feel the world for you
and I'll always remember this
even when I'm not with you.

WAYS TO SAY *I LOVE YOU*

I appreciate the ways you exist in this world.

Of all possibilities in the multiverse of realities, thank goodness I met you.

I feel so safe and at ease when we're together.

I think of you often when we're apart, and I cherish the memories we're making together.

You deserve everything you want in this lifetime and all the lifetimes after.

I'm so lucky to be part of your world.

I imagine us being friends throughout different eras of our lives.

I love learning about your dreams and your history.

I enjoy learning your love languages.

You teach me what it feels like to be loved and cared for.

I'm rooting for everything you want to be and do.

I believe in you! I really do!

Time with you feels healing to me.

I've dreamt of moments like this.

I want to be here with you.

●●●●●●●●●●●●●●●●●●●●●●●●●●●●●●●●●●●●●

THE VIEW OF YOU

Think of events that have had a significant impact in your life. What experiences have shaped you? Where have you lived, who have you loved, and what are the origins of your passions? Where have you come from, and how can this history support the direction you want to grow? Draw it out as a timeline to better appreciate all the life you've lived to get to here and now. The way you might marvel at the vastness of a canyon or the view of a setting sun across an ocean, admire the detailed picture of your life too.

●●●●●●●●●●●●●●●●●●●●●●●●●●●●●●●●●●●●●

THIS DREAMING

Dreaming is one of the most powerful elements of change. When we dream, we're connecting with the future and freeing ourselves from past limitations. Dreaming is also a practice of deep presence. As you notice changes in your life, look at the world through this renewed lens. Continue collecting evidence of different possibilities. Return to this section as you ride the momentum of growth and healing into a life that supports all of you.

TO MY INNER CHILD

dear baby
these limits were learned
this shame was taught

life is more than something to survive

remember—the first times you touched yourself
you listened to your body, you located your pleasure
you were disciplined for feeling good

between your legs became the fruit of temptation
forbidden, banished if touched

I learned: I am only as loved as I am good
I learned: feeling good is bad
suppress suppress
if you want to make it through the day

now we understand
what you felt was not a sin
it was an ability to wonder
to satisfy, to imagine

mommy said no
mommy said no
MOMMY SAID NO

remember—you found a CD
put it into the kitchen computer
watched the uncut video for "Right Thurr"
felt the pleasure pulse with each ass clap

mommy cannot see me watching this
mommy cannot see me sinning

church three times a week
indoctrinated me into obedience
indoctrinated me out of my pleasure

I read something that said:
the opposite of depression isn't pure joy
it's the ability to free your feelings
to feel it all without shame

don't forget 수지 (Suji)
one of great wisdom
your name a lifeline
your name a reminder
that you can learn
to be unafraid
of everything
that stirs within you

remember this place
remember this feeling
this is who you are meant to be

LISTENING TO INTUITION

Intuition is like a child. It wants to play make-believe. It has no regard for rules or logistics. It wants attention and appreciation. It thrives on simplicity and needs little to be happy.

With age, we neglect this child to focus on different responsibilities. Listening to intuition starts to feel like a luxury we can't afford.

Following curiosity is like letting this child place dots across the pages of your life. It's hard to tell what picture will eventually emerge, but there's no need to connect all the dots immediately. It will make sense over time.

As you practice change, each tiny shift contributes to this larger picture. If you have a sudden urge to try something you haven't tried before—go on a date with a new friend or cocoon for the weekend, maybe—listen and follow through. Each pleasure your intuition pursues becomes a mark on the map of your life.

MAPPING YOUR WAY INTO COMFORT AND EASE

Sometimes we can't give ourselves our most ideal form of care. When we're in the throes of depression, anxiety, or a meltdown, it's too hard to tap into "the wise mind" (a term from Dialectical Behavioral Therapy). Some questions I ask myself when I'm in these states:

- What is one small thing I can do to make my life easier right now?
- What is one tiny change I can make to relieve some stress?
- What has felt satisfying in past situations?

It's also been helpful for me to understand the roots of my discomfort. From there, I can map out what feels doable for me in any given moment. Using the chart on the next page as an example, note your current emotional or mental state, frustrations, and the conditions that impact you on one side; on the other, note some small actions that feel doable for you right now. Refer back to this list of comforts next time you're feeling stuck.

WHAT IS WITHIN YOUR REALM OF INFLUENCE?

FOR...	TRY...
DEPRESSION	planning something to look forward to, singing a song that matches your current mood, studying healing justice and trauma theories
ANXIETY	deep breathing, vagus nerve exercises, grounding touch with someone you love, naming your worries out loud and building a care plan around them
ADHD	reminding yourself what you're doing right now, listing reasonable goals for when you get distracted, not punishing yourself if you can't focus on just one thing, seeing a curiosity through
AUTISTIC FATIGUE	stimming, nonverbal communication, sensory breaks, sensory joy, sharing your access needs, setting boundaries with yourself and others, learning disability justice principles

I FELT THE FUTURE YESTERDAY

well, there's a war
there's a war here
and in countries
across the sea
there is a ration on hope
and this is a kind of survival
we didn't rehearse for

        well, there's a war
        gas prices are high
     inflation is the worst it's been

             and every
                movement
                   in history is
                     repeating itself

and still we have   places to go   and people to see   and memories to meet

I watched a film
about the multiverse
and felt myself there
(it's real! I knew it was real!)
which means there is
a version of me
somewhere with
everything
I ever wanted
which means if I

close my eyes and
map myself there
I can teach my body
how to feel the future

some days, it feels like everyone has forgotten me
some days, I forget to remember myself

SCRIPTING THE FUTURE

We are experiencing a massive paradigm shift. Astrologically, politically, socially, and environmentally, the world is changing at a dizzying pace. With crises and disasters that feel out of our individual control, it makes sense that manifesting has become a popular way of feeling like we have agency within our lives.

In Maxine Hong Kingston's *The Fifth Book of Peace*, she writes, "The reasons for peace, the definitions of peace, the very idea of peace have to be invented, and invented again. Children, everybody, here's what we do during war: In a time of destruction, create something. A poem. A parade. A friendship. A community. A place that is the commons. A school. A vow. A moral principle. One peaceful moment." Manifesting is a process of invention. We can create feelings, experiences, and worlds with our intentions and actions. When we feel helpless about all the destruction around us, the process of creation can help us connect to a sense of inner power.

Manifesting also lets us question society's arbitrary rules. Who made up these rules, and who do they help? What would it mean if we were all inherently powerful and worthy? What if manifesting our dreams can help contribute to a world with more equity and inclusion?

Using a technique called future scripting, write a journal entry from the future. Write about what you're doing and what fulfillment you've found. Write about how your day begins and what kind of activities fill your time. Write about what you're proud of, grateful for, and excited about. What kind of love do you experience? What kind of impact does your work make?

Write about your relationships with the people and environments around you. Write about what you've created as if it's already something alive in the world.

• •

IT'S NEVER TOO LATE TO CHANGE YOUR WORLD

I don't like the idea of "coming out." This language assumes that we're expected to be in hiding. At the same time, declaring "I'm queer!" over and over again is exhausting and in some situations, dangerous.

When I practice envisioning a liberated future for everyone, I think of a world free of two fixed genders and a binary—gay or straight—approach to romance. I envision a world where we can love without limits, a world that is inclusive and accessible by design, a world where we feel safe to be honest with one another, a world where no one has to "come out." I don't need the entire world to be aligned with this future—I can shape my life as a world of its own and surround myself with people who are committed to changing their worlds too.

Maybe you're in your thirties and exploring your pansexuality. Maybe you're in your fifties and curious about hormone replacement therapy. Maybe you're eighteen and embracing a genderqueer identity. Wherever you are, you're right on time. And as my friend Chella Man reminds me, we have the rest of our lives to make our dreams come true.

If you feel hungry for different people and different conversations, feed that hunger. If you find yourself dreaming and building alone, share your dreams with the people around you—physically or digitally—and see who resonates. Be vocal about what you want and what you're wishing for. Let your people find you. You will find your community, even if it's with one other person.

MAIN CHARACTER

it's hard for me to
watch movies with
white people as the leads
because that is not what
my life looks like
white people are not
the main characters

> my characters are
> Korean, Chinese, Vietnamese, Sri Lankan
> Black from Jersey, Black from St. Kitts
> Filipina from Hawaii
> Deaf, neurodivergent
> they/she, she/he/they
> queer, as in free to be
> someone different every day
> pansexual, as in everyone is lovable
> trans, in transition, transitioning
> gnc, nb, fluid, as in let's have fun with gender

so it's hard to see
white people
with limited
ideas of gender
take up space
on my screen
in my home
on my computer
on my TV

because it feels inaccurate
and it's hard for me to
sit through inaccuracy

which is why
I scroll for so long
looking for
stories to watch
because I find
most on my screen
offensively unrelatable

I was once in a
relationship with
someone who
didn't understand
why I cared so much
about representation

why I got so
excited when I saw
a Deadline headline
announcing a project
starring Asians
created by Asians
until one day
while searching
Netflix for something
to watch, he said

you're right
I don't see any Asians
your options are so slim

whoa, slimmer than slim
I'm sorry I didn't
see it sooner

and I said
yes, this is why we watch
so many Black films
because these characters
are more believable
more relatable
more accurate
and this is the closest
option I have
until more are made

hello Hollywood
can you please invest in our stories
(writers, directors, showrunners
producers, actors, editors, set designers
stylists, makeup artists, casting directors
THE FULL CAST AND CREW)

not that we need to be mined,
but you're really missing out
on a lot of gold*

---

* Sociologist Nancy Yuen, who is an expert on race and racism in Hollywood, consistently debunks the myth that there is no audience for Asian American stories. Through her, I learned that *Crazy Rich Asians* was the highest-grossing rom-com in a decade, and the seven-time Academy Award–winning *Everything Everywhere All at Once* is A24's most successful film to date. These statistics are important in making a case for more consistent investments in Asian American and Pacific Islander storytellers.

HOW TO KEEP LOVE ALIVE

1. Resist urgency.
2. Encourage autonomy.
3. Connect over common interests.
4. Be open to adventure.
5. Sit with uncertainty.
6. Grow apart, come back together.
7. Initiate novelty.
8. Celebrate softness.
9. Maintain multiple sources of comfort.
10. Prioritize safety.
11. Disagree without defense.
12. Do not build a world around one person.
13. Worlds are built together.
14. Welcome fluidity.
15. Shift codependent habits to interdependent habits.
16. People are not projects.
17. Study yourself too.
18. Save some stories for next time.
19. Celebrate the successes others might not notice.
20. Process the past just enough to keep moving forward.
21. Say yes to different forms of love, stay open to different ways of loving.
22. If you're afraid of what space will do, think of it as a portal to somewhere new.

EXPANDING YOUR CAPACITY TO LOVE

Moving homes and switching schools every few years prevented me from building a sense of security throughout my childhood and teenage years. I often felt isolated, and this isolation became a trigger for depression. Then, this depression made me feel irritated and ashamed—which caused me to isolate further. It's a vicious cycle that made me afraid to express love for people I might inevitably lose.

During the summer of 2020, I participated in a virtual workshop facilitated by poet Jenevieve Ting titled "Queer Love Is Spacious." Referencing scholar José Esteban Muñoz and his thoughts on queer futurity, Jenevieve opened my mind to a different way of loving. Instead of thinking about love as having a singular focus with a fixed destination, they proposed that when we queer the way we love, we are practicing our inherent spaciousness. Every time we practice love in a way that promotes autonomy and fluidity, we are learning how to love in a revolutionary way.

If this is true, there's no such thing as a waste of time or a loss of love, because our ability to love expands with every effort. Love is a muscle that becomes more powerful with practice. The more we show up to learn from love, the more lessons love will teach us.

Maybe our pain informs our intentions. Maybe our traumas shape the ways we care. When we love ourselves with depth and fluidity, we deepen and circulate the ways we love each other.

● ●

WHAT PARTS ARE HARD TO LOVE?

Is there a part of your body you've had a hard time loving? Or an aspect of your personality? Imagine these parts* of you as versions of the people you've been, trying to support you in the ways they know how. Write out what you would say to them, as the person you are now. What questions would you ask? How would you listen to them? What are they trying to say? How would you affirm them and remind them of their power to heal?

* For a supportive framework, read about the "Internal Family Systems Model" developed by Richard C. Schwartz.

● ●

WE PROTECT US

I've been rising in
love with myself lately
like I'm blooming
into my reality
like everything
around me is
dripping with
nectar
which makes me
less and less afraid to
taste my own sweetness

I feel like I'm
building paradise
around me
a paradise that
protects, nurtures
cares for those who
have not been
historically nurtured,
tended to, and cared for

love is the strongest form of protection
presence is the most potent form of medicine
this way, maybe we can build a world
so free, we don't need protection

"We protect us" is a rally chant created by organizers leading the movements for Black and
queer liberation.

A LOVE LETTER TO MY TRANS FRIENDS

maybe / they are afraid to love you because / you are from
the future / you are from a time when gender was as fluid
as age, as time, as home / how it was thousands of years ago
until hoarders decided to define and divide / maybe they are
afraid to love you because they see your freedom as a refusal
of their rules / they see your joy as a threat to the ways they're
married to their misery / maybe they are afraid to transcend this
illusion / to fully accept our intricacies and imaginations /
maybe they are afraid of the night / the sky / how dangerous it
seems when you're not among the stars / maybe they have
never known what it's like to make love in the moonlight

This poem was written after the Brooklyn Liberation march in June 2021, during which community leaders reminded us to not be complacent to the organized attacks on trans people in the United States.

1. From January 2021 to June 2021, more than 100 pieces of anti-trans legislation were filed in over 30 states. This is a state of emergency.

2. Twenty-seven trans people were murdered in the first 6 months of 2021. Forty-four homicides of trans people were recorded in 2020, with countless other incidents of transphobic violence unrecorded. We cannot accept this violence.

UNLEARNING TRANSPHOBIA

To address transphobia, we must be able to identify it. And while we've come to a point in American culture where saying something blatantly racist or sexist is largely considered unacceptable, many aren't as aware of what transphobia looks and sounds like.

In January 2023 as I write this, there is an alarming amount of anti-trans rhetoric making its way into American legislation. Trans rights are being systematically attacked. Trans leadership, trans stories, and trans education are more important than ever if we are to build a future that is safe and supportive for trans youth and trans adults.

If you're unsure where to start, *Disclosure* is a documentary executive-produced by Laverne Cox that outlines the impact of transphobia in Hollywood films. For a global perspective, *Transnational* is a docuseries from Vice News that follows trans people around the world and explores the daily discrimination they face.

It's important to note that, just like racism, heteronormativity, and ableism, transphobia is so prevalent in our culture no one has escaped its influence—it requires active undoing.

Journal with honesty about what you're unlearning around what it means to be trans. Make a strategy to learn from more trans voices and write down any trans artists, leaders, and thinkers whose work you admire.

SELF-PORTRAIT AS A SEA ANIMAL

a poem about being neurodivergent

Everyone is moving faster than me, and that's okay.
Everything moves slower for me, and that's okay.

Time is an illusion we bend for our own making,
and I tend to make meticulous movements for my own safety.

Sometimes I stay under rocks for longer than I should,
if I'm measuring shoulds by how hungry I get.

I am always a little hungrier than my stomach is full.

It's hard to eat when eating is a
competition that requires muscles
and I—to be clear—am made mostly of jelly.

While others use their fins and tails
to swirl through the water,
I have learned to use what I have.

My expertise is in floating, in widening my look
at this earthly ecosystem and fitting
myself into the puzzling nature of survival.

I am not a shark, I do not hunt.
There are no movies made about me.
Mostly because I can't communicate.
But when I find the language,
I'll have stories to tell.

When it's time, ask me about the waves!
Ask me about the direction of the wind,
the way it sweeps us in dizzying circles even
when we're a hundred feet underneath the ground.
Ask me about where it's taking us, what we have to
look forward to and what we have to look out for.

When floating is all you can do,
you become part of the current.

And this—this slowness,
this silence—is the speed of my sea.

A NEURODIVERGENT WAY TO RUN A RACE

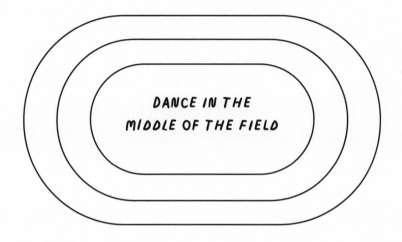

DANCE IN THE
MIDDLE OF THE FIELD

VISUALIZATION FOR SELF-ACCEPTANCE

Stretch out your limbs. Let your body take up space, from side to side and top to bottom. Imagine yourself rooted in the ground and lifted by the sky. Slowly roll your neck, shoulders, and hips around. Move between these positions for a few breaths and vocalize any sounds that want to come out of you.

Breathe, even if your mind worries or wanders.

Imagine looking at yourself in a large mirror. The room around you is glowing with soft purple and orange light. Take a few moments to observe yourself.

Notice the thoughts that come up and the sensations you feel. Do not judge any of them as good or bad—just observe.

If you notice any harsh thoughts, acknowledge them as you turn their volume down. You have creative control over your inner dialogue.

Now, try tuning into any thoughts that feel supportive and turn that volume up. What thoughts within you feel kind, true, and caring?

Breathe into these thoughts and give them a shape. Maybe they're tiny stars. Maybe they're holographic bubbles. Maybe they're golden confetti. Imagine these thoughts showering around you, landing on your skin, absorbing into every part of you.

Remember, you are powerful in ways you've yet to experience. You are allowed to feel good in this body you're in, right here, right now. You are allowed to move at a pace that feels appropriate for you. You are allowed to forgive yourself, want yourself, and tend to yourself.

Allow these reminders to support you as you move through the rest of your day.

Before you end this practice, thank yourself for showing up for the work of loving and accepting all of you.

● ●

● ●

MIRROR MEDITATION

Find a mirror; ideally, do this at home with minimal distractions.

Play music or sounds that help you feel calm and peaceful.
Silence is okay too.

Look into the mirror and connect with what you see. Take as long as you need to feel fully connected to your reflection.

Let your eyes wander to anything that calls your attention. What do you think about what you see? What do you notice about this person you're looking at?

Write down any observations or insights that come up.

If you're blind or low vision, you can do this meditation through touch. Sitting or standing in a position that feels good for you, touch each part of your body as slowly and intentionally as possible, working from the top of your body to the bottom. As you breathe and connect with yourself, notice the thoughts that come up. You can record your observations in a voice note as you're doing the practice or set aside time afterward to process your experience.

● ●

ON LIKABILITY

sometimes, I think I have not lived enough
living as in mistaking, fumbling
rebelling against authority
I wonder whose choice this was—
my mother's, for demanding behavior
so rigid I feared anything that bent
outside her definition of purity and godliness
or mine—for not disobeying her enough

in pre-k, Miss V places a toy traffic light
at the front of the classroom
red means silence, yellow means whisper,
green means talk with your inside voices

the traffic light is meant to teach discipline
the traffic light represents the rules

mostly, I admire Miss V and
I want her to admire me back

one day while the light is set red
a classmate asks me a question
I respond back in my yellow voice
Miss V interrupts me mid-sentence
calls my name like a kettle's hiss
I still carry this memory in my bones
the embarrassing sensation of being caught
of being bad, of breaking the rules
breaking *her* rules

it's hard to decipher if this inclination
for rule-following stems from being
raised as a girl, by a migrant Korean
mostly driven by fear, rarely joy
little luxury to ambition beyond
surviving day to day

with age, I'm arriving at an understanding
엄마 didn't have the insurance of safety
following the rules of good Christian
good wife, good daughter
meant minimizing the violence
obedience was a choice made for her
so maybe she didn't know the choice of
disobedience was possible for me

and this taught me to hold my tongue
before someone else could grab it from me
because censoring myself
at least put me in a position of control

speak only when spoken to
speak only when it is guaranteed
to be safely received
only when your words
will contribute to your likability

my therapist tells me my intuitions are reliable
that at one point, my intuitions were twisted signals
of keeping myself safe in unsafe environments
but now, I have enough wisdom

to trust my intuition safely
I'm safe here, I keep telling my body
until we believe it

I am untwisting likability
from my personality
practicing the art of disobedience
in service of my inner authority

this is my new game of survival

THIS MANY WISHES

the yoga teacher says
you can be amazing
without being perfect
four bird bodies
swan diving
under a steel structure
in a place someone
(a colonizer?)
named Storm King
who inhabited this land*
originally, we wonder

this, a collaborative rest
where we synchronize breaths
and let the city melt off our backs

afterwards we frolick
watch each other
run and roll
up and down the hills

gusts of wind make
dandelion seeds
mate mid-air

I think, quick—
what's my wish?
I think, slow—
each seed, a wish

to have more than enough
resources, support, energy
to live a life of wonder and rest

I think, this makes more sense
we are always allowed
this many wishes

* Land acknowledgment is a practice of bringing awareness to the original inhabitants and stewards of the land we occupy. Centuries of colonization and industrialism have disconnected us from Indigenous wisdom about how to respectfully connect to the places we live in and honor the resources we consume. As the climate crisis deepens in severity and urgency, learning from Indigenous teachings can help us reorient our relationship to the land, supporting the survival of our generation and future generations to come.

LET LOVE BE LOUD

be loud about love
let it be overheard
kiss six times in public
declare the ways
this person has changed you
keep some moments private
some secrets secret
but if love wants to spill
pour it out, give it away
how else do we learn
how to treat each other
how else do we learn
this is the adoration
we always deserved

walk each other to
the bathroom, wait
until they're done
share a plate of food
sit skin to skin
nuzzle neck to neck
text each other *"I'm home safe"*

be a resting place
permission to unbutton pants
let belly hang
burps escape
without apology

say the thought
you're afraid to think
say the sad out loud
make it smaller
make the joy bigger
than it could ever be alone

be loud about love
let others listen in
know that they too
are looking for this
and they too want to know
this love—this mighty of love,
this length of love—exists

and this love is waiting for you too

LOVE LIKE IT'S THE MOST IMPORTANT WORK YOU'LL DO IN YOUR LIFETIME

My love is loud. It spills out of me like marbles, and I'm not good at waiting to tell someone how I feel. I don't think cards should be reserved for birthdays, and I'll often send lengthy texts to friends when I feel enamored by their presence in my life.

Being neurodivergent comes with social stigmas and systemic challenges, but it also comes with an audacious ability to think and feel deeply. My friends often tell me I'm one of the most affirming people they know, because I'm not afraid to express what I'm thinking as I'm thinking it. I'm not afraid to share my love.

Everyone—and especially people who are queer, Black, Brown, and/or disabled—absorbs messages that they're not enough. Friendship is where we can remember our strength, where we can remind one another we are beautiful and worthy and talented. As the world works to harden us, friendship is where we soften. Friendship among people who have been marginalized, oppressed, and systemically excluded is an act of revolutionary, world-building love.

Ableism teaches us to keep it in. Stick to the script of what's acceptable, what's expected, what will cause the least disturbance. Often, these expectations to present as "normal" mean masking our inner world to conform to an outer illusion. This is similar to code-switching and involves physical and psychosomatic tension that can cause both short-term and long-term damage to the body.

There's so much we can learn from neurodivergent ways of communicating: practicing honesty (even when it's uncomfortable), removing the pressure of performance, prioritizing what our bodies need, and being firm about the support we deserve.

If love wants to be shared, get out of its way. Let it be expressed without ego, without expectations. This, too, is liberation work.

HOW TO SHOW UP FOR THE LABOR OF LOVE

Sometimes I think about caring for my friends as a job. Not in a dreadful, obligatory kind of way. But in a way that acknowledges care as a form of labor.* It takes work to maintain relationships, and I value the intimacy I've built with my friends just as I value the foundational work that has built my career. What if we got creative about the way we love our friends?

How do you like to be loved? What expression of love feels easy for you? Here's a list to get you started. Add to it with practices that resonate with you.

1. Make a note on your phone for each of your closest friends.** Include their special interests or passions, favorite foods, allergies, birthdays or astrological signs, memories of them you cherish, and any other essential information you can think of. Make note of any lessons they've taught you, as well as any quirks or characteristics you admire. This is especially helpful to return to in times of conflict.

2. Write a letter to your friend for no particular occasion and give it to them the next time you meet. Tell them about the last time they made you laugh or how you feel when you think about them. Express to them why you cherish your friendship or tell them about an experience you're excited to share. Or express these feelings in a collage or artwork for them.

3. If you feel like you're drifting from a friendship, check in. Some ideas for how to do this:

- "I feel like we haven't talked in a while and I really miss you. Do you have some time for a 1:1 soon?"
- "I'm really craving some time with you. What does your week look like?"
- Send a photo or video of a sweet memory together. "Thinking about this day and how fun it was. I want to go on another adventure soon!"
- If you know your friend doesn't have a lot of capacity, offer something you have capacity to give. Order them a meal or make one and drop it off. Ask if there's anything you can take off their plate, like helping with laundry or scheduling appointments. Or simply remind them what they're good at.

* I was first introduced to this concept from Leah Lakshmi Piepzna-Samarasinha's book *Care Work: Dreaming Disability Justice.*

** This practice was inspired by my friend Kimberly Drew, who is diligent in the way she learns how to love people the way they want to be loved.

• •

CYCLE OF COMMUNITY CARE

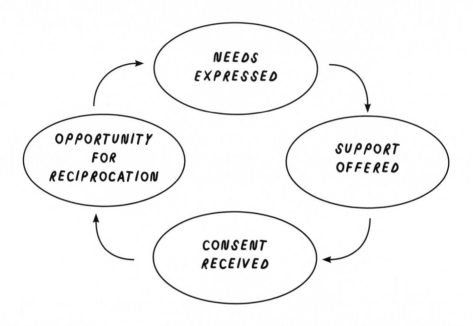

We have to build relationships that are stronger than our institutions.

— adrienne maree brown

SOFTER TRUTHS

1. You are a story in motion. No need to rush the reveal.
2. You are your most important source of permission.
3. Enduring through the ugly can help deepen the beauty.
4. Three deep breaths are three spiral-steps back to center.
5. Maybe it's not about outgrowing the shadows and pains of our past.
6. Maybe it's about learning to become familiar with these feelings.
7. Surely, we deserve to feel the other side of our fears.

MAPPING INTIMACY

Community care is a way of tending to one another's needs in ways our larger social and political structures fail to do. Community is a network of relationships, always shifting, adapting, and growing. This wasn't something I always had access to—it's something I've intentionally built over time. My sense of community has changed drastically as I've become clearer about my values, sharpened my vision of the world I want to live in, and realized the importance of disability justice. In her blog *Leaving Evidence*, writer and educator Mia Mingus* uses the term "access intimacy" to describe the feeling of safety and closeness that happens with someone who understands your needs as a disabled person. This language helped me think of community not as the people with whom I have the most in common, but as the people with whom I feel the most intimacy. I feel access intimacy when I'm getting sleepy inside a loud bar and my friend gives me his shoulder to rest my head on. I feel access intimacy when I'm having a lonely night and my friend stays on the phone with me while I fall asleep.

Using a set of concentric circles, map out the people you are building or want to build more safety with. You might feel different levels of vulnerability with different people and that's okay. Refer back to this map whenever you feel lonely or when you're wondering who you can reach out to for support.

* Mingus's concept of "pod mapping" is another framework for understanding community connections and levels of intimacy.

AVENUES OF INTIMACY

(How to find community)

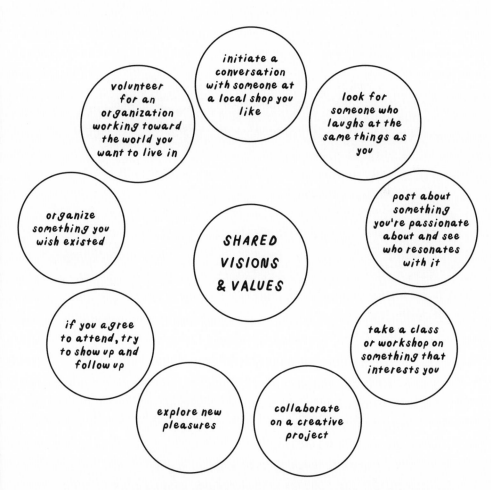

Community-building (verb): developing and sustaining relationships with people we can practice access, inclusion, and liberation with. Community-building is how we can source models of hope and healing. Through community, we learn how to repair from conflict, respond to crisis, and imagine a more livable future.

WHAT IF

what if I walked
    what if I walked
        without a destination
            what if I kept going
                what if I stopped
                    looked at the sky

what if I imagined the sky
    as the glass of a globe
        what if I imagined
            the rain as snow
                what if I let myself
            wander through the weather
        what if I held my own hand
    like a prayer
what if I turned to myself
    like the god I was
        raised to believe

    thank you thank you thank you
        a 13th century mystic
            named Eckhart once said
        if the only prayer you
      ever said was thank you
      that would be enough

what if I belonged here
    within this body
        within this vessel I've built
    art from Asian, queer artists
memories stamped on my skin

what if I looked at myself
    both reflection and prism
        what if I remembered that no one,
            not a single person no camera
        from any angle no device
    no matter how advanced
no form of audience
    or surveillance
        could ever see me
    the way I see myself
        from this position
            looking down
                at my chest
                    at my torso
                        at my stomach

            nobody can see me
        the way that I do
    so why am I so cruel
to something
    so exquisite

what if I
    turned this apology
        into a celebration
            what if I
                transformed this table
                    into a moving vehicle
                    a convertible
                        wind blowing hair
                            sun on skin

what if the sun
comes from within
what if I'm ignoring
the galaxy within me

take note of this weather, too

what if I

let the stars

in me come alive

burn as they were
meant to

what if I

let myself emit

what if I

dazzle as freely

as the sun persists

what if, this whole time

I've been waiting for permission to exist

what if?

● ●

YOU ARE YOUR BEST HEALER

We deserve support and care as we heal. But something I've learned as I've worked with shamans, body workers, reiki practitioners, and therapists is that I am my own best and most important healer. When I go see a healer, they're not healing me; they're holding space for me to heal myself. I am most familiar with my pain and I am most equipped to know what medicine I need.

Specialized healthcare, holistic medicine, and alternative healing practices are inaccessible for most people. Without ample time, energy, and money it can be impossible to navigate our (racist, sexist, transphobic, ableist) healthcare system, much less explore different paths. Taking control of your own healing is often the most available remedy.

What are you healing right now? Write a letter to yourself. Extend compassion for the changes you're experiencing and the challenges they're bringing up for you. Tune into your inner wisdom by taking deep breaths, closing your eyes, and moving your body in a soothing way, and write down whatever comes to mind without trying to censor it. Let your inner guide heal you.

● ●

SENDING FLOWERS TO YOUR SIDE OF THE MOON

I love the way you

> leave the door open while you pee
> fall asleep next to me
> let me say a protection spell before you leave

I love the way you

> read scripts with me
> lead me through the crowd
> knowing I can't see as much as you

you teach me what it feels like to be free!

I love every just because
a call to say hello here was my day
a share of good news
a showing me a corner of your room

<u>I want to hear all your bells</u>

> the noisy
> the scary
> the terrible and untrue

I can't promise I'll always answer

> my mind is loud on its own

> but I'll always be listening   *from my side of the moon*

if I leave before midnight
call me in the morning

> tell me what I missed
> tell me about the cuties you kissed

you are becoming one of my favorite memories
and I hope to all the gods
we keep moving alongside each other

here, take these flowers
to your side of the moon

This poem was written during Annika Hansteen-Izora's "Reimagining Love Letters" workshop with Writer's Club NY on February 12, 2022.

WE GET BETTER AT ANYTHING WE PRACTICE

In January 2020, a few months before the pandemic put us into a lockdown, I was in Portland, Oregon, browsing through New Renaissance Bookshop looking for something that would help me change my life. I felt disconnected from my passions and disassociated from my body, unhappy with the life I was living. Almost a year into a job as a Diversity Equity Inclusion Lead that I had pitched and created for myself at an advertising agency, I wasn't sure why I still felt unfilled. On paper, I was living a life of purpose. I was getting paid to create and execute a strategic vision to build a more equitable company. It was my "dream job," but I still felt this aching in me like I was missing something.

I stumbled across a book called *Creative Visualization: Use the Power of Your Imagination to Create What You Want in Your Life* by Shakti Gawain. It felt like a message from the universe, an arrow pointing to the answers I was looking for. This book was my introduction to visualization, a practice of imagining myself within scenarios of satisfaction and fulfillment. Many sections in this book stem from my passion for visualization and how I use it as a tool to design my future.

During the first year of the pandemic, visualization led me to resign from my advertising job and pivot to consulting, public speaking, facilitating, educating, and creative work.

One day during a visualization practice, I imagined myself singing on a theater stage. My closest friends were in the front row cheering me on while I shimmered below bright lights, singing the final note of a triumphant musical number. Then, tears. Involuntary, uncontrollable tears. A sign.

I asked myself what this could mean. Was I talented enough to sing for an audience? How could I make this happen, when it seemed so out of reach? The first step seemed obvious: practice. I found a vocal coach and began taking weekly lessons over Zoom. Weeks turned into months turned into years, and I improved. I started to hit higher notes with more ease, my vocal cords loosened, and I now sing with more confidence, less concerned about how "bad" I sound.

Maybe there's something in your life that you want to do. Maybe this something—a skill, a talent, a goal—feels out of reach. Remind yourself that progress comes with practice. Practice visualizing your future. Practice pursuing your passions. Practice being part of a community. Practice loving yourself the way you want to be loved. This is how we get better—not through immediate mastery but through persistent, steady movement. What practices are calling to you?

The questions we ask become the stars we follow.

> — *Josh A. Halstead in* Extra Bold: A Feminist, Inclusive, Anti-racist, Nonbinary Field Guide for Graphic Designers

THIS TIDE, THIS TIME

I endured all this way to tell you

you can make it through
I promise you

LEVITY LOADING

1. I felt it all.
2. The heavy almost drowned me.
3. I became hungry for laughter.
4. I tried to give in to gravity.
5. I learned how to live with it.
6. Yes, even that time I said that stupid thing
   at that stupid time at that stupid place.
   (Applaud every attempt.)
7. I placed it somewhere safe.
8. I tried so many times I dug a new way.

As an alternative, indulge in reality TV.
Don't think too much about it.
Enjoy without analyzing why you enjoy it.

EACH ONE A MEMORY

starfish above wrist

> you are one of one
> no one else in the
> shape of you

galactic yin yang

> duality is in nature
> don't resist your gravity

jellyfish below elbow

> 6 weeks spent in a gym
> learning about rhythm and rhyme
> strangers became family
> you love this shit!!!
> try this more, follow your flow

empress on horse, left arm

> the shaman said
> there's a warrior within you

garden door, right arm

> queer love is a portal
> to unlock a different future

reflective sphere

> if you're going to mirror
> be a disco ball

sleeping sloth in tree

> resting is your most important job
> the pace you need is right for you

music note, right foot

a decade of training

there will always be a dancer within you

LOVE AS A RENEWABLE SOURCE OF ENERGY

A history of harm and neglect can crush our faith in love. In my daily healing practices, I sometimes feel like I'm going in circles until I notice a difference in the ways I'm giving or receiving compassion and care.

We need to know what intimacy feels like in order to experience intimacy with ourselves. The same way we need food and fuel to sustain our bodies, it's okay to need love to sustain the health of our heart.

I believe in love as a movement. I believe that love can change us if we let it. I believe we heal in the ways we are held. Hurt people may hurt people, but loved people also love more. In this way, love is the most renewable source of energy.

WE HEAL IN THE WAYS WE'RE HELD

we heal each other   *change the cycle*
by resting in each other's softness   *leave room for surprise*
by savoring one word after another   *for plot twists!*

we heal each other
by the gravity of our generosity
by letting love escape from hiding   *what are you afraid to say here?*

an organizer for Black liberation
taught me the Hawaiian practice
of reconciliation and forgiveness
      hoʻoponopono: *I'm sorry, please forgive me, thank you, I love you*

            we can become comfortable with apologies,
               see them as portals to deeper connection

we heal through witnessing
each other's ugliest, staying
through the messy
                  though we are allowed
                  to leave and this does
                  not make us a villain

we heal each other
by allowing our
still unknown
not fully formed
to be seen
to be sensed
to be supported

we heal each other
through the pauses
please, don't perform
kindness / it already
lives within you
without your performance

it is so easy to love you

if you're not there
not yet ready
to meet there

do not worry
we can move
in parallel paths together

we heal in stillness and solitude   we heal in movement and connection
we heal by listening   we heal by expressing
I'll love you right where you are   *there's no rush, I'll wait with you*
if you need to go to the bathroom   *if you need to slow down*
if you change your mind   *if you need me to repeat*

community can exist as one

                    there are so many layers of yourself to meet

community can exist as two

           if conversations are my favorite creative practice,
                  community is an artform too

we heal in the ways we hold each other
we heal in the ways we hold ourselves

this is how we heal   *this is how we heal*
this is how we heal   *this is how we heal*

MEDITATION TO FEEL GOOD

Get settled into your body. Breathing deeply, take your time and locate an area of your body that feels tight, tense, or uneasy. If there are multiple areas, focus on one that feels tender to you.

Focus your breath as if you're breathing in and out from this part of your body.

Keep breathing with this. As you relax into the practice, imagine yourself having a conversation with this part of your body. What is it saying to you?

Sit with this question for as long as you need until a word, memory, or insight shows up. You'll know you've found it when it feels calm and sure. If it helps to deepen a sense of relaxation, imagine yourself lying under a tree by a bright green pond. Here, there's no rush. There's nothing for you to do and nowhere else for you to be. Here, there's only the sound of birds singing, leaves rustling, and water flowing. All the elements around you are supporting you to feel good.

Sit with whatever surfaces. Keep breathing, lengthening your exhales. Resist any urge to take action on the insight or to think of this information as a problem that needs a solution.

Thank this part of your body for communicating with you. Ask if it has anything else it wants to share. Listen again with the patience you would give to someone who is learning something new. With practice, you'll find insights come clearer and quicker.

With each message, send thanks. Your body is a complex ecosystem that keeps your gut digesting, your heart pumping, and your brain operating. Take some more time to acknowledge the intricate body you're in and appreciate the ways it supports you to do all that you're doing.

When you're ready to come out of the meditation, slowly scan your environment and return to a pace of breathing that feels natural to you. Write down anything you want to remember and take the time you need to be ready to interact with the world around you again.

This meditation was inspired by sessions with my somatic coach Casey Llewellyn. To get the benefits of being guided through this meditation, you can ask a friend to read this aloud to you. Another way to experience this is to record your voice reading it aloud and listen with meditative music playing in the background.

● ●

• •

WHAT DO YOU BELIEVE?

If you've gotten to the end of this book, you are meeting a different version of yourself than when you started. You've taken yourself through different portals of imagination, challenged binary ways of thinking, and explored different ways to dream about the future.

Remember, change is a lifelong practice. It's a journey with moving destinations and no singular outcome—a shape-shifting road map to endless discoveries.

What values will guide you? What influence will you have on others? What will you have said with the life you've lived when you've reached the end of your time?

Write a statement of belief to direct your path moving forward. Think of it as a manifesto of sorts of how you intend to navigate the world.

Use the below as an example.

I believe I exist on purpose, with purpose.

I believe every person has a right to a dignified life,
a life abundant with what they need.

I believe I can contribute to changing the conditions
that prevent us from this life of abundance.

I believe in exploration and experimentation.

I believe we get better at anything we practice.

I believe change is possible because change is always happening.

*I believe the future is what we make of it and I believe
enough people care to make the world a softer, sweeter place to live in.*

I believe softness is a strength.

I believe sweetness is a form of medicine.

I believe anything is possible if we say it is.

I believe I can live the life I want to live.

● ●

ACKNOWLEDGMENTS

For as long as I can remember, I've been committed to change, growth, and evolution. I think part of this is because I care about the collective and part of this is because change is what helps me survive. There's an autistic term called "penguin pebbling," which means the giving of tiny gifts as a way of showing affection. I like to think the universe was pebbling me with teachers in the form of books, art, conversations, and other resources when I was looking for ways to change the conditions of my life. To everyone who has shared their lineage of thought at conferences, community meetings, workshops, and in 1:1 dialogue: thank you. These pebbles have helped me build frameworks and develop practices to heal from the impact of living in this body, in this time. I would not have been able to move through the laborious process of writing, selling, and editing a book—and take care of myself through it all—without people showing me how.

I thank all the movements I'm a student of, and all the people who've shaped the teachings of these movements. Studying the Asian American movement of the '60s and '70s taught me the importance of solidarity—advocating for those who have been historically marginalized and seeing how our struggles connect and intersect. Studying the queer liberation movement and the impact of the 1969 Stonewall uprising taught me that direct action and mutual aid are critical elements in supporting queer life. Studying transformative justice taught me that everyone deserves love and forgiveness and that everyone is redeemable. Studying abolition taught me that crisis happens in a culture designed to harm many and protect few, so we must learn to create protection and care in ways the government fails to. Studying disability justice taught me that punishing ourselves into productivity is a product of racist, capitalist ableism and building access into the way we design the future is something that helps everyone live a more dignified life. Studying the neurodiversity paradigm taught me that we are allowed to move at our own pace and that there is nothing inherently wrong with who we are, how we learn, and what we need to feel safe and connected.

Feeling the impact of these movements is why I believe in the power of change and the importance of community. To every friend who has supported my dreams, spoken the language of care with me, listened to me talk about the conception and iterations of this book: thank you. To Kimberly Drew, for speaking an encyclopedic level of love languages, for reminding me that dreaming big is a superpower, and for showing me that shame has no place in friendship. To Chella Man, for teaching me the practice of living within a continuum, persistently leading with love within a disability justice framework, showing me the transformative power of access intimacy, and inviting me to read some of these poems at the closing of "PURE JOY: 14 Disabled Visual and Performance Artists" at 1969 Gallery in August 2022. To Yannik Stevens, for being a pillar of safety and impeccable taste, and for being a sounding board who witnessed multiple iterations of this book with enthusiastic support. To Sarah Burke, for showing up for me during times I didn't know how to show up for myself, for demonstrating the power of political engagement, and for loving me with fierce, unwavering patience. To Mohammed Fayaz, Oscar Nuñez, and Adam Rhodes, for dedicating a decade of labor and intention into Papi Juice and creating spaces for NYC's QTPOC to gather and build community. To Sammy Kim, Nick Andersen, Stevie Huynh, West Dakota, Angela Dimayuga, DeVonn Francis, Vincent Chong, Rohan Zhou-Lee, and everyone who supported organizing efforts for Protect Asian Lives in April 2021. This gathering became a portal into QTPOC community in NYC and changed my life completely. To Jenevieve Ting, for welcoming me into the worlds they've built, for showing me what it feels like to experience radical, revolutionary queer Asian friendship and community, and for reigniting my love for poetry. To Jess X. Snow, for encouraging me to keep writing when I wasn't sure if my work was "good enough" and for listening to me read many of these poems out loud over the course of our friendship. To Jalena Keane-Lee, for manifesting with me during full moons and reminding me that ambition is not something to be ashamed of. To Thanu Yakupitiyage, Jenny Yang, Ashley Osborne, Frank Wong, Mengwen Cao, Mary Kang, Poppy Liu, Coco Layne, Sean Miura, Jay Blacks, Warren Jones, Jamila Reddy, Alyza Enriquez, Mar, Keith Lafuente, Yên Sen, Denny, Ben Flores, Kia Damon, Tara Aquino, Al Ittelson, Zeba Blay, Maya Margarita, Jason Niu, Sara Elise, Kevin Gotkin, Jen White-Johnson, and every friend who reminds me that love is abundant and I'm never moving through life alone.

To Bianca Wilson, for introducing me to meditation, aromatherapy, emotional freedom technique, and so many other tools I've incorporated into my healing practices. Watching you show up for the work of getting to know yourself over the past ten years has been a continuous source of inspiration.

To my best friend in the entire world, Mike Bautista, for being in my life—for a decade and counting—and being someone I've always felt immediately at peace with. The way you live is a lesson in living freely, joyfully, and diligently. You are my soulmate, one of the first people I came out to, and someone I can be fully unmasked with. I love you forever.

To my mother and sister, whose artistry and resilience will always be embedded in the ways I move through the world. To Aunt Linda, Aunt Cindy, and 이모, for helping raise me into who I am today.

To Fariha Róisín, whose class "Writing with Vulnerability" helped me write with more bravery, which helped birth many of the poems in this book.

To Gavriel Cupita-Zorn, for your affirmations and encouragement during our weekly writing sessions, and for the insightful prompts that helped birth many of the pages in this book.

To every change and healing-oriented teacher, healer, organizer, facilitator, and fellow student in all the learning spaces I've been a part of over the past decade. To my vocal coach Dave Klodowski, somatic coach Casey Llewellyn, and the therapists I've worked with throughout the years, for helping me connect to my voice, my body, and my inner world.

To Richie Keo, Moe Lamstein, and Butterfly Cayley at Community New York, for supporting my growth as an artist across multiple mediums. To Annie Hwang at Ayesha Pande Literary, for teaching me about the publishing process, championing my voice, helping me grow as an author, and guiding this book through multiple versions until it reached its perfect home. To Allison Adler, for the thoughtful, honest, laborious ways you helped sharpen the contents of this book; to Pamela Geismar, for meticulously and beautifully designing the layout; and to the publishing team at Chronicle Prism, for helping this book reach the readers it's meant to reach. To Jocelyn Tsaih, for channeling the cycles of change into the cover artwork.

And to you, for believing in change, spending time with my stories, and loving yourself enough to dig deeper toward a more loving world within yourself. May you find all the care, support, and community you need to feel free.

RESOURCES AND ADDITIONAL READINGS

Mental health, wellness, and disability justice resources

Therapy for Queer People of Color (therapyforqpoc.com)

National Queer & Trans Therapists of Color Network (nqttcn.com)

Neurodivergent Therapist Directory (ndtherapists.com)

Inclusive Therapists (inclusivetherapists.com)

Therapist Neurodiversity Collective (therapistndc.org)

Fireweed Collective (fireweedcollective.org)

Project LETS (projectlets.org)

Call BlackLine (callblackline.com)

Sins Invalid (sinsinvalid.org)

Access Is Love (disabilityintersectionalitysummit.com/access-is-love)

Disability Visibility Project (disabilityvisibilityproject.com)

Leaving Evidence (leavingevidence.wordpress.com)

Community Resistance Intimacy Project (criproject.com/resources)

Alt Text as Poetry (alt-text-as-poetry.net)

So You Think You're Autistic Resource Guide (bit.ly/autisticguide)

Crip News (cripnews.substack.com)

The Embodiment Institute (theembodimentinstitute.org)

New Earth Mystery School (maryamhasnaa.com/new-earth-mystery-school)

California Institute of Integral Studies (ciis.edu)

The following is a list of what I was reading while writing this book. I'm thankful for the works of these writers, whose thoughts helped shape my own.

The Collected Poems of Audre Lorde

How to Carry Water by Lucille Clifton

Passion by June Jordan

Dictee by Theresa Hak Kyung Cha

Time Is a Mother by Ocean Vuong

When I Grow Up I Want to Be a List of Further Possibilities by Chen Chen

Your Emergency Contact Has Experienced an Emergency by Chen Chen

DMZ Colony by Don Mee Choi

Litany for the Long Moment by Mary-Kim Arnold

The Trees Witness Everything by Victoria Chang

Alive at the End of the World by Saeed Jones

The Dream of a Common Language by Adrienne Rich

The World Keeps Ending, and the World Goes On by Franny Choi

How to Cure a Ghost by Fariha Róisín

A History of My Brief Body by Billy-Ray Belcourt

Poukahangatus: Poems by Tayi Tibble

My Baby First Birthday by Jenny Zhang

No Knowledge Is Complete Until It Passes Through My Body by Asiya Wadud

Content Warning: Everything by Akwaeke Emezi

Dark Testament and Other Poems by Pauli Murray

Thirst by Mary Oliver

Sister Outsider by Audre Lorde

Living for Change by Grace Lee Boggs

Cruising Utopia by José Esteban Muñoz

How to Write an Autobiographical Novel by Alexander Chee

No Country for Eight-Spot Butterflies by Julian Aguon

Getting to Center by Marlee Grace

Beyond the Gender Binary by Alok Vaid-Menon

Continuum by Chella Man

This Is What I Know About Art by Kimberly Drew

The New Queer Conscience by Adam Eli

The How by Yrsa Daley-Ward

People Change by Vivek Shraya

You Are Here (For Now): A Guide to Finding Your Way by Adam J. Kurtz

How We Show Up: Reclaiming Family, Friendship, and Community by Mia Birdsong

Goodbye, Again: Essays, Reflections, and Illustrations by Jonny Sun

Crying in H Mart by Michelle Zauner

What My Bones Know by Stephanie Foo

The Chronology of Water by Lidia Yuknavitch

Parable of the Sower by Octavia E. Butler

On Earth We're Briefly Gorgeous by Ocean Vuong

Blackspace: On the Poetics of an Afrofuture by Anaïs Duplan

Black Futures by Kimberly Drew and Jenna Wortham

Creative Visualization by Shakti Gawain

Transitions by Julia Cameron

We Will Not Cancel Us: And Other Dreams of Transformative Justice by adrienne maree brown

Emergent Strategy: Shaping Change, Changing Worlds by adrienne maree brown

We Do This 'Til We Free Us: Abolitionist Organizing and Transforming Justice by Mariame Kaba

The Racial Healing Handbook: Practical Activities to Help You Challenge Privilege, Confront Systemic Racism, and Engage in Collective Healing by Anneliese A. Singh

My Grandmother's Hands: Racialized Trauma and the Pathway to Mending Our Hearts and Bodies by Resmaa Menakem

Unmasking Autism: Discovering the New Faces of Neurodiversity by Devon Price, PhD

Taking Off the Mask: Practical Exercises to Help Understand and Minimise the Effects of Autistic Camouflaging by Hannah Louise Belcher

Care Work: Dreaming Disability Justice by Leah Lakshmi Piepzna-Samarasinha

The Future Is Disabled by Leah Lakshmi Piepzna-Samarasinha

Disability Visibility by Alice Wong

Demystifying Disability by Emily Ladau

It's OK to Feel Things Deeply by Carissa Potter

Extra Bold: A Feminist, Inclusive, Anti-racist, Nonbinary Field Guide for Graphic Designers by Ellen Lupton, Jennifer Tobias, Josh A. Halstead, Leslie Xia, Kaleena Sales, Farah Kafei, and Valentina Vergara

Radical Dharma: Talking Race, Love, and Liberation by Rev. angel Kyodo williams, Lama Rod Owens, and Jasmine Syedullah, PhD

The Way of Tenderness by Zenju Earthlyn Manuel

On Freedom: Four Songs of Care and Constraint by Maggie Nelson

The Magic of Manifesting by Ryuu Shinohara

How to Love by Thich Nhat Hanh

Answers from the Heart by Thich Nhat Hanh

Becoming Supernatural by Dr. Joe Dispenza

Body Work by Melissa Febos

The Drama of the Gifted Child: The Search for the True Self by Alice Miller

No Bad Parts: Healing Trauma and Restoring Wholeness with the Internal Family Systems Model by Richard Schwartz, PhD

JAY BLACKS

ABOUT THE AUTHOR

Jezz Chung is a writer, actor, and public speaker who studies change, movement, and performance. They make art about their experiences being alive as an autistic, disabled, queer Korean American, and their work has been shared by millions of people around the world. They believe in the healing power of friendship and imagination as a portal to liberated futures.

Jezz has lived in Georgia, Texas, and California, and is now based in Brooklyn, New York. *This Way to Change* is their debut book. You can follow along as they dream out loud @jezzchung across social media, learn more about the work they do at jezzchung.com, and read about the worlds they're building at jezzchung.substack.com.